Using Complexity Theory for Research and Program Evaluation

POCKET GUIDES TO
SOCIAL WORK RESEARCH METHODS

Series Editor
Tony Tripodi, DSW
Professor Emeritus, Ohio State University

*Determining Sample Size:
Balancing Power, Precision, and Practicality*
Patrick Dattalo

Preparing Research Articles
Bruce A. Thyer

Systematic Reviews and Meta-Analysis
Julia H. Littell, Jacqueline Corcoran, and Vijayan Pillai

Historical Research
Elizabeth Ann Danto

Confirmatory Factor Analysis
Donna Harrington

*Randomized Controlled Trials
Design and Implementation for
Community-Based Psychosocial
Interventions*
Phyllis Solomon, Mary M. Cavanaugh, and Jeffrey Draine

Needs Assessment
David Royse, Michele Staton-Tindall, Karen Badger, and J. Matthew Webster

*Multiple Regression with Discrete
Dependent Variables*
John G. Orme and Terri Combs-Orme

Developing Cross-Cultural Measurement
Thanh V. Tran

*Intervention Research:
Developing Social Programs*
Mark W. Fraser, Jack M. Richman, Maeda J. Galinsky, and Steven H. Day

*Developing and Validating Rapid
Assessment Instruments*
Neil Abell, David W. Springer, and Akihito Kamata

*Clinical Data-Mining:
Integrating Practice and Research*
Irwin Epstein

*Strategies to Approximate Random
Sampling and Assignment*
Patrick Dattalo

Analyzing Single System Design Data
William R. Nugent

Survival Analysis
Shenyang Guo

*The Dissertation:
From Beginning to End*
Peter Lyons and Howard J. Doueck

Cross-Cultural Research
Jorge Delva, Paula Allen-Meares, and Sandra L. Momper

Secondary Data Analysis
Thomas P. Vartanian

Narrative Inquiry
Kathleen Wells

Structural Equation Modeling
Natasha K. Bowen and Shenyang Guo

*Finding and Evaluating Evidence:
Systematic Reviews and Evidence-Based
Practice*
Denise E. Bronson and Tamara S. Davis

*Policy Creation and Evaluation:
Understanding Welfare Reform in the
United States*
Richard Hoefer

Grounded Theory
Julianne S. Oktay

Systematic Synthesis of Qualitative Research
Michael Saini and Aron Shlonsky

Quasi-Experimental Research Designs
Bruce A. Thyer

*Conducting Research in Juvenile and
Criminal Justice Settings*
Michael G. Vaughn, Carrie Pettus-Davis, and Jeffrey J. Shook

Qualitative Methods for Practice Research
Jeffrey Longhofer, Jerry Floersch, and Janet Hoy

Analysis of Multiple Dependent Variables
Patrick Dattalo

*Culturally Competent Research:
Using Ethnography as a Meta-Framework*
Mo Yee Lee and Amy Zaharlick

*Using Complexity Theory for Research and
Program Evaluation*
Michael Wolf-Branigin

MICHAEL WOLF-BRANIGIN

Using Complexity Theory for Research and Program Evaluation

OXFORD
UNIVERSITY PRESS

Oxford University Press is a department of the University of Oxford.
It furthers the University's objective of excellence in research, scholarship,
and education by publishing worldwide.

Oxford   New York
Auckland   Cape Town   Dar es Salaam   Hong Kong   Karachi
Kuala Lumpur   Madrid   Melbourne   Mexico City   Nairobi
New Delhi   Shanghai   Taipei   Toronto

With offices in
Argentina   Austria   Brazil   Chile   Czech Republic   France   Greece
Guatemala   Hungary   Italy   Japan   Poland   Portugal   Singapore
South Korea   Switzerland   Thailand   Turkey   Ukraine   Vietnam

Oxford is a registered trademark of Oxford University Press in the UK
and certain other countries.

Published in the United States of America by
Oxford University Press
198 Madison Avenue, New York, NY 10016

© Oxford University Press 2013

All rights reserved. No part of this publication may be reproduced, stored in a
retrieval system, or transmitted, in any form or by any means, without the prior
permission in writing of Oxford University Press, or as expressly permitted by law,
by license, or under terms agreed with the appropriate reproduction rights organization.
Inquiries concerning reproduction outside the scope of the above should be sent to the
Rights
Department, Oxford University Press, at the address above.

You must not circulate this work in any other form
and you must impose this same condition on any acquirer.

Library of Congress Cataloging-in-Publication Data
Wolf-Branigin, Michael.
Using complexity theory for research and program evaluation / Michael Wolf-Branigin.
p. cm. – (Pocket guides to social work research methods)
Includes bibliographical references and index.
ISBN 978-0-19-982946-0 (pbk. :alk. paper)
1. Evaluation research (Social action programs)   2. Social
service—Research—Evaluation.
3. Social service—Evaluation.   4. Complexity (Philosophy)   I. Title.
H62.W622 2013
001.4—dc23   2012026858

1 3 5 7 9 8 6 4 2
Printed in the United States of America
on acid-free paper

Contents

Preface vii

1 Introduction: The History and Theory of Complexity 1

2 Framing Social Services as Complex Systems 32

3 Research and Evaluation Methods for Complexity 49

4 Shifting from a Metaphorical to a Mathematical Approach 60

5 Social Work Applications of Complexity 77

6 Introduction to Agent-Based Modeling 94

7 Developing Agent-Based Models 114

8 Concluding Remarks and Proposed Research Agenda 131

Appendix A. Coding for Example 1: Travel Training for Persons with Disabilities 151

Appendix B. Coding for Example 2: Housing Patterns for Persons with Disabilities 157

Appendix C. Example of an Agent-Based Model Report 164

Appendix D. Additional Resources 170

Glossary 174

Notes 179

References 182

Index 195

Preface

Before entering academia, I worked as a social service administrator. Like many colleagues, I put great effort into program evaluation; however, too often these efforts had only minimal impact on documenting improvements, influencing decisions, measuring outcomes, and sustaining programs. Using my two decades of experience working in various social service situations, I wrote this book in order to envision and conduct social program evaluation differently. It applies a complexity theory paradigm that emphasizes systems thinking to assist in identifying why clients seek services from an organization, what maintains their interests and involvement, and evaluates their outcomes through inquiry into the emergent collective behavior that results from their interactions with others and their environment.

My first social work experience began during the final year of my undergraduate program in sociology and psychology. The project I worked on arose from the bottom up, as a few local social workers were seeking a new way for persons with intellectual and developmental disabilities (who had been institutionalized) to become fully participating members of their community. The project sought to develop a living model for this population that could be replicated, as the recently enacted state mental health code called for increased community inclusion. This early experience taught me the value of respecting the perspectives of the persons served, while introducing me to how a few individuals can create social change within the overarching guidelines of legislation.

Throughout my professional and academic career, I had an interest in research methods and advanced statistical approaches. My dissertation applied spatial autocorrelation to how individuals with disabilities had housing patterns that could be either random or not. Without knowing it, this was my initial academic foray into complexity. More recently, I realized that pursuing a complex systems approach to social work involves identifying the underlying patterns and structures across phenomena using mathematical formulas. An early exposure to this occurred as I came across the concept of gravity models applied to urban planning where the mass (the number of people in a given region), multiplied by the frequency of trips in and out of the region, were calculated to estimate the need for services.

About five years ago as a tenure track faculty member, I was searching for an area of study to coalesce my multiple research interests. Before my academic career, I had worked in substance abuse treatment, corrections, housing programs, and in services for persons with intellectual disabilities. Creating a cohesive research agenda based on these disparate foci became problematic. To add another level to this quandary, my real interest was to advance an innovative theoretical framework that could improve social work practice, research, and evaluation. I decided to frame my research agenda on a few books I had read over the previous summer. The first was *Emergence* by Steven Johnson (2002), which introduced the notion of how ants, slime molds, neuroscience, and urban environments shared similar characteristics.

Upon returning from summer break, and during the orientation for our incoming class of master of social work (MSW) students, faculty members were asked to describe our research interests to these eager students. I spoke of how the self-organizing behaviors of various organisms, such as ants, slime molds, and birds, were relevant to social work education. A few colleagues were curious how slime molds related to social work. I believed that such an approach could open new paths for how we, in the long term, conceptualize social work, because each set of these organisms displayed ways to organize without any central authority. Many of my colleagues likely thought that this was a bit odd, but I pursued the topic of complexity anyway, believing I was on to something.

Over the next few years, it became apparent that applying complexity to social work would require a few books written by social workers, and these books had to be aimed toward a social work audience for the paradigm to become useful (e.g., Hudson's *Complex Systems and Suman Behavior, 2010*). While sitting at my desk, surrounded by piles of books and articles on complexity theory, I ask myself, why another book? The answer is simple, as none of these really address how social work researchers, evaluators, administrators, and graduate students can approach the new scientific paradigm of complexity. Therefore, this book provides examples of how it has been applied to social work concerns; applies the material to specific social work issues; uses existing and emerging statistical and modeling approached; and sets a course for future endeavors.

The research and evaluation methods discussed will provide a foundation for using complexity as a tool to identify order in what appears to be chaos. Finding order in chaotic situations often appears an unreachable goal; just enter the records office of a social service center that has yet to digitalize their client records. Yet in this book I ask whether understanding complex social service phenomena can be as easy as:

1) Knowing your clients' or organization's current functioning level;
2) Identifying what attracts a client or organization;
3) Understanding how other clients and organizations then self-organize;
4) Seeing how this leads to an emergent collective behavior that in turn leads to anticipating changes and adaptation;
5) Identifying and understanding the trends and outcomes that result from social service interventions.

I ask this question through the lens of the research paradigm known as complexity theory. Complexity theory is consistent with the emerging constructs known as new science (Wolfram, 2002) or the science of the twenty-first century. As is true in other academic and professional disciplines, complexity will play an increasingly prominent role in how social work as a discipline evolves.

An essential aspect to grasp early in the discussion is that complexity relies on basic or conceptual inquiry into the tenets of complexity theory and complex adaptive systems. As will be described in detail, these tenets, or related concepts—including the wisdom garnered from diverse perspectives and heuristics, self-similarity of activities (whether conducted at the micro or macro level), and self-organization—provide promising avenues for inquiry.

Social workers were early adopters of general systems theory, ecosystems theory, and have applied cybernetics in the quality improvement efforts conducted within most social service organizations. We have lagged other academic and professional disciplines in adopting complexity as an organizing framework and paradigm for future inquiry. Applying this paradigm will foster innovative approaches that use computational methods and new media to encourage social change.

Social workers assumes a person-in-environment perspective; however, the dominant research methods we use focus on linear approaches that provide limited information and insight concerning others involved in our clients' lives. This book seeks to address this void by introducing various contemporary statistical approaches—social network analysis, agent-based modeling, spatial analysis and related methods—to address this emerging research perspective. Agent-based modeling contrasts to traditional research methods because it uses individual level data to build models rather than the top–down reductionist approach that aggregates behaviors. Systems dynamics modeling is related because it uses feedback as an essential component, but differs because it aggregates behaviors of individual agents. This is why a text that applies this emerging paradigm specifically to social work research and evaluation is needed.

Writing this book required reviewing a large amount of theory. While some students do not appreciate fully the role of theory, especially as it relates to research and knowledge development, it allows us to generalize our knowledge across situations. Therefore, a major purpose of this book provides social workers with an introduction to a theoretical organizing framework that can be applied across multiple settings including clinical, administrative, policy practice, community oriented, or research/evaluation.

Perspectives on what complexity theory is and how it applies differ from one researcher to another. This book suggests one perspective of applying this paradigm. The materials covered are not intended to give the reader a comprehensive background to complexity, but rather to introduce the main concepts and provide a cohesive pathway using several social work applications. I have seen the frustration over the past few years of other social work faculty members and researchers that similarly see complexity as a promising paradigm. These colleagues have expressed how difficult it has been to get manuscripts using complex systems accepted for publication. In fact, I received one comment from a top-tier social work journal with the comment, "…complexity, don't we want to make evaluation simple?" That manuscript was not accepted by that journal.

Social workers operate within a swirl of data, and this provides a further reason for this book as it centers on making sense out of this overwhelming amount of information. This is addressed by presenting a framework for creating order from these apparently chaotic environments, and to assist program planners and administrators improve their decision-making. Applications include making decisions within social service organizations, managing contracts, managing data and information, improving outcomes, addressing accreditation, and improving relations with stakeholders. Whereas the majority of research studies within the social work directly attempt to measure the impact of an intervention on a sample of participants, there are often larger scale interventions that also require the demonstration of a quantifiable improvement. I explore the application of appropriate qualitative and quantitative methods in order to address this issue.

I sincerely believe that social work as a discipline benefits by applying the more rigorous mathematical concepts to which we were exposed in elementary and secondary school. To understand complexity theory and how complex phenomena are expressed, we need at minimum a rudimentary understanding of set theory, game theory, logic, and graph theory. These concepts are introduced and applied to social service situations. As this book was developed, national efforts to increase education in science, technology, engineering, and mathematics (STEM) have increased. My hope is that this book at a minimum begins to assist social work students to begin thinking about research as more than the customary courses we take in bachelor of social work (BSW) and MSW programs.

The intended audience for this book includes PhD students in social work, and social work researchers and evaluators. This may serve as a supplementary text for a course in research in graduate social work or related health and human service curricula. The major problems instructors encounter in these two courses is providing an undergirding framework through which students can frame their intervention and evaluation practice. The major student obstacle involves understanding the interconnectedness between systems operating in their current and prospective clients' lives.

Recently, social work research coursework has tended toward evidence-based practice, and this is essential in developing valid and replicable interventions; however, students often lack the larger context. With the adoption of new paradigms, it remains essential to maintain your practice behaviors consistently with the values, skills, and knowledge embedded within the social work profession. In writing this, I assumed that readers would have completed at least two research courses that included both qualitative and quantitative methods, and at least one class in advanced statistics. The material is by no means exhaustive, and where appropriate, additional resources to provide greater depth are suggested.

When conceptualizing this book a conundrum arose, should I as a social worker use the resources within our university community for several aspects of this volume (especially on agent-based modeling), or should I use an emergent approach whereby students and research assistants support me in explaining the material? I chose the latter and, as a result, I believe the materials are presented in a more understandable approach that remains applicable and accessible for graduate students and for researchers within our discipline. Unlike other volumes in this series from Oxford University Press, this one uses a larger amount of theory because complexity will be new to most readers.

Given my long-standing interest in studying nonlinearity in social service research and evaluation, expressing the material became a very nonlinear, complex, and difficult process. But it was quite enjoyable, because it forced me to develop a cohesive understanding of a topic that was important to me. It provided an opportunity to work with a great group of individuals. Ironically, this book conflicts with complexity because the materials are presented in a somewhat linear manner. If it were correctly oriented, influences would be simultaneously occurring from many directions. It seeks to give the reader the needed background to fully understand this diverse topic, but most readers will benefit by referring to the additional resources, links, and in essence, the networking tools provided to understand and apply this approach.

Several people helped immensely in developing this book. My wife, Karen, also a social worker, assured that the work was oriented toward actually helping people, and was not simply an intellectual exercise. Jakob Klaus, a graduate research assistant who has worked with me for the past two years, was instrumental in finding much of the information provided in this book. He helped me to create the agent-based models, and coauthored chapter 7. My colleagues in the Department of Social Work and the College of Health and Human Services at George Mason University provided vital support and comment on early drafts. Several graduate research assistants over the past four years gave valuable support including Timothy Donahoe, Hannah Kane, Amanda Shapiro, Elizabeth Shuman, Hisako Sonethavilay, and Mark Taylor. Of course, the editors and staff at Oxford University Press, including Nicholas Liu, Tony Tripodi, Maura Roessner, Lynda Crawford, Nisha Selvaraj, and the external reviewers, Who all were instrumental in assuring the manuscript was cohesive and readable.

As I began developing, winnowing, and revising these pages, I thought I understood how complexity applied to social work. Readers—most likely graduate students beginning an academic career—will understand that they are complex adaptive systems. In writing the book, I realized how difficult and complicated an idea this whole emerging approach to complexity-oriented inquiry has become. My sincere hope is that reading this volume serves as an introduction to complexity theory and that you will use it as a beginning point for understanding complexity as a research paradigm, and as a tool in developing research skills based on complex systems.

Using Complexity Theory for Research and Program Evaluation

1

Introduction: The History and Theory of Complexity

The first chapter introduces the concepts of complexity science (often represented as complex adaptive systems) and explains how this line of inquiry developed over the past six decades. The roots of complexity science are reviewed with a description of how it emerged and reached paradigm status. Complexity has achieved this paradigm status in both physical and social science disciplines, and provides theoretical underpinning for fields including communications and linguistics. Complexity, however, has yet to achieve a similar status in social work.

The study of complexity arose because a group of scientists believed that complex systems—across many natural, societal and technological domains—shared similarities. This includes being adaptive, self-correcting, and emergent. In this book, I apply these similarities to social work settings and suggest a usable framework for incorporating complexity theory to evaluate social programs. The first chapter traces the beginning of this emerging field of inquiry and introduces related concepts often found in complex systems that are relevant to social work research and evaluation.

Covering the broad topics of both evaluation and research in a single book can become cumbersome. To introduce potential users to the paradigm, both research and evaluation are discussed because recent applications have addressed social program evaluation issues, while research aspects of complexity remain conceptual. For the sake of brevity, I am assuming that the chapters oriented more toward evaluation will be somewhat less technical, whereas the research-oriented chapters involve a deeper understanding of methodology. Readers will find that chapters 2 and 3 are applicable to both evaluation and research. Chapter 4 is more oriented to research, but still provides theoretical foundations for evaluation. Chapter 5 is oriented toward social work evaluation, and chapters 6 and 7, because of their focus on computational modeling, mostly apply to research. Please note that chapters 6 and 7 provide only an introduction to agent-based modeling. Program evaluators with advanced methodological skills may find these chapters to be of interest, too. Chapter 8 ties the approach together for both research and evaluation purposes and suggests several future foci.

After completing the first chapter, readers should gain

- an understanding of the historical antecedents in social work that lead to adopting a complex systems orientation;
- an understanding of the differences between complexity theory, chaos theory, complex systems, and complex adaptive systems;
- an initial understanding of several concepts related to complexity theory that are present within social work.

PURPOSES

Understanding what complexity theory is and how this new paradigm can be applied to social work research and program evaluation can be daunting. To make this accessible in a small volume, the purposes of this book include

- providing an alternative research paradigm for social workers to consider and use;
- introducing this paradigm by explaining the concepts behind it and the components that comprise complex systems;

- providing research and program evaluation contexts in which this paradigm is applicable for social work inquiry;
- introducing agent-based modeling (ABM) as one method for understanding complex systems;
- suggesting research directions to pursue for social workers who are interested in complexity theory.

As social workers, we see social service delivery as complex systems. This has only become apparent to me for the past few years after delving into the vast literature on this emerging scientific paradigm. To most of you, the term complex systems may sound vague, but it is in fact a well-defined construct with many lines of inquiry (see Figure 1.1). Much value will be derived by reading and working through the exercises found at the end of each chapter. They will introduce you to a language used by other disciplines, and suggest how this approach can affect social change.

So what is complexity? We assume that it is more than statistical interactions, more than the networks that represent our connectedness, beyond the Gestalt Therapy tenet that the whole is worth more than the sum of its parts, and more than the multiple levels within structures (whether organizational or social). Complexity as a research paradigm has roots in the area of nonlinear dynamics (how a system changes over time through a process that uses feedback to continually inform that system) and includes several components focusing on the interconnectedness of individuals and aspects within their environments. Complexity theory inquires into the influences, connections, and decisions that people make and how these influence an emerging group behavior. Three issues are paramount to understanding what comprises complexity: self-organization, feedback, and emergent behavior. These three issues provide the primary foci in the succeeding chapters.

Although complexity theory evolved within the natural sciences, it serves as an approach for understanding the interactions of networks of services, and the evolution of policies and services within our discipline. Following social work's long tradition of framing social behavior in the social environment using systems theory, recent alternative schemes based on postmodernism and quantum mechanics arose. These schemes support the notion that outcomes from social work interventions were unpredictable (Pozatek, 1994). This initial foray into nonlinearity, however, tended to focus on chaos and not complex systems (Campbell, 2011).

Complex System Components
- Agent-based
- Heterogeneity
- Iterative Processes
- Feedback
- Boundaries
- Self-organizing
- Emergent Behavior

Concepts Related to Complex Systems
- Bordering between Chaos and Equilibrium
- Conflict/Cooperation
- Diverse Perspectives
- Diverse Heuristics for Problem-Solving
- Niche Construction
- Robustness and Resiliency
- Self-similarity
- Scalability

Applications and Methods
- Developmental Evaluation
- Network Analysis

Figure 1.1 Layout of Book.

Complexity theory serves as a complementary or alternative approach to traditional experimental-based research. As will become apparent, complexity can be found in many aspects of research, as evidenced by recent federal funding initiatives and scientific literature that call for stronger links to public policy, whereby the direction comes from the bottom up (Gans, 2011). Rather than using hypotheses testing as the basis for determining effectiveness, rigorous complexity-based research often uses agent-based modeling created to simulate environments through computer intensive techniques and replicate the interactions of individuals (*agents*). Based on these agent-level activities and interactions with others, it becomes possible to study the layers of emergent behaviors produced by agent-level interactions.

Conceptual studies in complexity theory directly relate to long-established assumptions in social work. Important underlying concepts, such as diverse perspectives, robustness, and cooperation, play a vital role and will be discussed in several stages. Intuitively we understand and appreciate these concepts, and the results from quantitative studies during the past two decades that support how these concepts provide social benefits. For example, as explained by Hasenfeld (2010), we see the benefits of mutual social worker–client well-being because such mutual dependence likely encourages mutual respect and trust. When this mutual respect and trust is lacking, social services stratified in terms of power result.

SOCIAL WORKERS AS FOLLOWERS OF COMPLEXITY

In an odd twist of fate, social workers have followed an approach that for decades has been espoused by the field of theoretical physics. We were early adopters in applying and understanding the influences that networks and surrounding environments have on individuals, families, and communities. We operate in a world where it is common for people with diverse backgrounds to seek support from others with a similar need; where the initial concerns of a few active citizens can ignite social movements; and where neighborhood residents unite to resolve or alleviate disparities in their community. Although it may not have been previously apparent, all of these examples share the presence of self-organization and emergence. These components—self-organization and emergence—suggest an introduction to understanding how complexity theory and social work relate. Self-organization reflects the coming together of change agents for a common cause while emergence reflects their generated outcome.

Similar to public health and urban planning, modern social work arose from the rapid urbanization during the final decades of the nineteenth century. Like these other disciplines, we recognize the importance of relationships with others as expressed through interconnectedness and the resulting networks. We acknowledge and espouse the benefits of individuals being interconnected with others and their surrounding environments. Certainly most social scientists, urban planners, and public health practitioners agree. Jane Jacobs (1961), the noted urban critic, provides an early commentary on the complexity of urban environments. In her efforts to save lower Manhattan (Soho) from planners (e.g., Robert Moses) who focused on what was perceived as a rational approach to urban renewal following World War II, she argued that such modernist urban planning rejected the city, because it rejected human beings living in a community. She appreciated a community, characterized by layered complexity, that appeared to be chaotic. This chaos represented the life and the entangled relationships that individuals had with others in their community. These interconnections and entanglements served to support others and provided vibrancy.

Social workers may easily grasp concepts from emerging research and evaluation approaches that focus on community engagement, such as empowerment evaluation, as many of these approaches seek to obtain grassroot input and action. For example, empowerment evaluation follows a stepwise problem-solving process such as that proposed by Andrews, Motes, Floyd, Flerx, and Fede (2005), whereby community workers approach social change by organizing for action, building capacity for action, taking action, refining action, and institutionalizing action. For practitioners and researchers from other disciplines, this may not be so intrinsic.

Suggesting that interconnections were not essential to healthy environments would contradict social work's person-in-environment (PIE) tenet. Other disciplines now follow our lead by realizing the importance of these surrounding influences. We see this in a recent initiative emanating from two of the great thinkers of complexity theory at the Santa Fe Institute (the world's premier institute centered on complexity). Physicists Bettencourt and West (2010) proposed a new science of cities wherein issues such as scalability are assumed and a "grand unified theory of sustainability" is envisioned. Their model for a new science included three characteristics: (1) less space needed per person as city size increases; (2) accelerated economic activity leading to higher productivity; and (3) diversified economic and social activities leading to more independence and greater creativity. We appreciate the interconnectedness of people and their environments through the use of general systems theory and ecosystems theory. Complexity expands on this framework by providing a means to further understand consumer and organizational interactions. Our discipline benefits from the basic research on the tenets of complexity. These tenets (referred to as the related concepts)—including wisdom garnered from diverse perspectives and heuristics, self-similarity of activities at both the micro or macro level, and self-organization—provide promising avenues for inquiry and teaching. For example, in social work, the concept of empathy parallels diverse perspectives, because we seek to understand how others see and understand a variety of situations.

Resources for conducting social work research and evaluation will likely remain level or diminish in the near future, as financial support for social service programs from governmental units and, to a lesser extent, private foundations is unlikely to expand significantly. Creating computational simulations to generate and model social work phenomena, based on existing and retrievable data, affords a potentially cost effective and robust approach for supplying decision makers with salient information.

Complexity theory serves as a complimentary research approach to evidence-based practice. Developing, evaluating, and disseminating scientifically supported approaches garners broader support for our field; however, multiple layers of knowledge are difficult to realize with traditional research methods (Adams, Matto, & LeCroy, 2009). Vast amounts of the published literature assume that distributions have normal distributions, when in fact these assumed normal distributions rarely occur (Micceri, 1989). As a research paradigm, complexity will not solve all problems, but rather it provides an orientation, with agent-based modeling being but one method. This will be reflected in the logic of the chapters as they are explained. Rather than testing hypotheses, in a complexity approach we simulate a generated observable pattern using the fewest number of plausible decision rules (Gilbert, 2008). Yes, I believe that we unknowingly have been users of this framework, but we failed to formalize its implementation.

Complexity is concerned with relationships and the interconnectedness of people. In writing about community organizations, and noted as early as in 1948, social work practice addressed the problems in the relationships between human personalities and the social environment (Pray, 2003). Pray warned about adopting a model where the social worker entered a community with the objective of curing its ills, rather than working in collaboration with its members. This collaborative approach permeates the delivery of services that we conduct in partnership in diverse social work settings.

COMPLEXITY, COMPLEX SYSTEMS, AND COMPLEX ADAPTIVE SYSTEMS

While complexity theory has become an accepted paradigm within the natural sciences, its assumptions pose significant challenges to social work research and evaluation. When applied, it typically has taken a metaphorical orientation (Cronbach, 1988; Holland, 1998). Complexity related articles have only appeared in the social work literature for the past dozen years (Bolland & Atherton, 1999; Hudson, 2000, 2004; Stevens & Cox, 2008; Trevillon, 2000; Warren, Franklin, & Streeter, 1998).

Having knowledge of systems thinking serves as an antecedent for understanding how complexity applies to social work. When using systems thinking in evaluation and research, three terms—systems thinking, dynamic complexity, and action research—overlap. According to McCaughan and Palmer (1994), understanding how a system operates involves systemic questioning, and they propose five prompts to understand dynamic complexity within a system. The first involves establishing circuitry: when agent X does something, what does agent Y do? What does agent X do next? The second prompt seeks to establish patterns over time, so that repetitions occur. The third explores meaning: what common meanings do behaviors have? Finding these common meanings provides for a form of pattern recognition. The fourth prompt seeks to explore the underlying or covert rules: what explicit and assumed hidden rules govern behavior in the system? Finally, the fifth prompt explores time dimensions: how do delays affect the system's behavior?

Dynamic complexity refers to situations in which cause and effect are subtle and often hidden. Social service organizations can be viewed as systems containing interconnected planning functions, control functions, technical expertise, and behaviors. Within these systems, the resulting subtle changes over time reflect dynamic complexity, and can arise in either complex or simple systems that exhibit multiple causes and effects resulting from the system's performance. Where dynamic complexity occurs, applying systems thinking aids in understanding how a social service system is held together through the various relationships and interdependencies.

The study of complex systems relies on iterative processes (the application of a function repeatedly so that the output from one iteration is used as the input to the next), and therefore shares characteristics with the well-known action research methods. As a corollary, Homan (2011) states several principles underlying participatory action research (PAR). First is the conduct of action research that is intended to deepen understanding; these actions lead to transformed relationships both inside and outside of the community. This includes open and closed systems which are prevalent in social service delivery. People who are affected in the community play central roles in conducting the PAR. Information generated through the PAR becomes a source of wealth in the community, and the process has the intention of building power for the community. The work is collaborative; it requires self-examination through cycles of self-reflection and adaptation (combining and winnowing). The PAR process, unlike experimental and quasi-experimental research, is based on hypothesis-generation rather than hypothesis-testing. It uses reliable and valid techniques and concludes with a critical analysis of findings. A broad distribution of findings is suggested to inform key stakeholders and other constituents.

Terminology used in a complexity (or complex systems) line of inquiry can be confusing. The terms complexity theory, complex systems, and complex adaptive systems will be used throughout. Complexity theory will refer to the overarching theoretical framework involving these related concepts. Complex systems will refer to the applications or environments in which the interacting components of complexity theory occur. Complex systems arise out of the individual interactions of agents that produce an emergent behavior, and where the system itself may not adapt, but the agents comprising the system do. In a manner similar to how ecosystems theory differs from general systems theory, CAS are complex systems that adapt in response to their environment (Page, 2011) and exhibit behavior whereby the system itself changes (adapts) in response to the evolving feedback provided.

Instances of direct application and a discussion of the necessary methodologies for investigating and applying complexity in social service systems have received limited coverage in the social work literature. A related literature, however, has emerged that addresses the concept of social innovation. Westley, Zimmerman, and Patton (2006) identified how interconnectedness leads to social change. The boundaries of this evolving literature reach beyond social work to include diverse disciplines such as international development, business administration, economics, and public policy. Social work was an early adopter of general systems theory, and applied cybernetics in the maintenance and improvement of social service organizations by building feedback mechanisms into program improvement activities; however, it has been late to adopt complexity.

Complexity provides a promising route for social work to have a unifying theory. For the sake of clarity, social services describe primarily not-for-profit organizations or governmental units that provide a series of interventions designed to address one or more needs of the individuals seeking assistance. These organizations typically receive funding from a combination of government sources, foundations, and donations. Such organizations exist in overlapping systems. Social program interventions typically are evaluated using a top–down approach, in which achievement of overall program objectives defines the success of a program. Consequently, the emergent behaviors resulting from micro-level interactions of individuals and their family units rarely receive attention. Having been influenced largely by the desire for generating evidence-based practices, social work research in recent years has increasingly focused on group comparisons. Integrating diverse research and evaluative methodologies based on the commonly used linear relationship and group comparison approaches into a coherent evaluative strategy, however, requires that the methodologies be sensitive to time and location.

General systems theory—the undergirding framework under which the social work profession operates—provides a framework for understanding essential PIE interactions through genograms and eco-maps (McGoldrick, Gerson, & Petry, 2008). Complexity builds and complements social work's PIE tenet. General systems theory as applied to social work leads to ecosystems thinking, as it inquires into the reciprocal relationships occurring across and between different levels of systems, where these levels of systems include individuals, families, communities, or organizations. This framework poses difficulties as we quantify such relationships and other social work phenomenon over time and location. This disparity has called for social work research oriented toward nonlinear approaches, such as spatial analysis, cluster analysis, and social network analysis (Israel & Wolf-Branigin, 2011).

Applying a complex systems approach to direct services—that largely were designed from knowledge gained from the social sciences—poses an even greater obstacle: it often uses a metaphorical approach for qualitative program evaluation activities (Holland, 1998). The metaphorical application of complexity provides useful insights into understanding that social service delivery systems function as complex systems. Framing complexity metaphorically serves as a useful step and is the basis of the next chapter.

Complexity is often confused with chaos theory, where randomness appears to prevail. Complexity theory and chaos theory comprise the study of nonlinear dynamics, and are useful for studying how phenomena change over time (Warren, 2008). Chaos theory provides a framework for inquiry into how simple systems may change unexpectedly, whereas complexity theory looks at how systems comprise numerous and interacting components. Complexity more accurately refers to underlying structures that upon initial review appear random, but that in effect display an underlying pattern. When I was a doctoral student, we were expected to observe the dissertation defenses of fellow candidates. A typical question posed by one member of the dissertation committee was whether the student plotted the residuals from their data, and what pattern, if any, became apparent? Without intention, this became an early exposure to complexity, the search for patterns within what appears to be randomness. Realizing that residual errors that initially appeared to be simply noise or error could indeed have some pattern, gets to the point of what the study of complexity involves.

DEFINITIONS OF COMPLEXITY

Complex systems and complexity are difficult terms to define. After digesting a large serving of books discussing complexity, no single definition exists. A few authors even consider viewing complexity not as a singular theory, but rather as a macro theory (Kelly, 2010; Mitchell, 2009). To provide some structure to the discussion, Page (2011) offers four definitions, including statistical complexity, residing between order and randomness, effective complexity, and Kolmogorov complexity. As you review these definitions, please be reminded of the importance of the previously stated components of self-organization and emergence.

The first, statistical complexity, proposed by Crutchfield and Young (1989), supposes that an algorithm can be created to classify existing data so that it can produce patterns that are similar to what the original data represented. This idealized search for indistinguishable patterns from the original data, however, is difficult to achieve.

The second definition proposed by Wolfram (2002), states that complexity resides somewhere between order and randomness. According to Wolfram, complexity represents neither simple patterns nor randomness, but instead, longer and interesting structures. These structures are not in equilibrium as characterized by fixed points or recurring patterns. Because they are not in equilibrium, they are chaotic.

The third definition, Kolmogorov complexity, refers to the minimum length of a computational program that will generate the desired set of characters or symbols. The noted Soviet mathematician, *Kolmogorov's* statistical version of complexity, also referred to as algorithmic information content, applies the concept of description length: the set of data can be represented by a string of characters or symbols from a defined alphabet.

The fourth definition, effective complexity (Gell-Mann & Lloyd, 1996), modifies the Kolmogorov definition and refers to the length of nonrandom information in a system. It measures the content of the regularities in a system. This approach seeks to remove randomness. The focus is on what information remains once the randomness has been eliminated. What remains is the description length, or the minimum amount of data that is required to communicate the essential information.

For our sake, we will use the definition based upon which a complex system exists. As noted already, scientific authors such as Gleick (2011) propose narrow definitions of complexity focusing on mathematical concepts based on formal communication theory. For our discussion throughout this book, our definition of complexity will be more generic, using the description of a complex system proposed by Mitchell (2009).

> A network of components with no central control and simple rules of operation that give rise to complex collective behavior, sophisticated information processing, and adaptation via learning or evolution. (p. 13)

You may notice that the term "complexity" has been replaced by the term "complex system." This will be discussed a bit later, but for clarity purposes, complexity exhibits itself within complex systems, and therefore the shift. The first piece of the definition, *network,* refers to the interconnected individuals present in a social system. The terms, *having no central control and simple rules,* suggest the self-organizing behaviors of individuals in social systems. The *collective behavior* is the result of the interactions and simple rules. The *information processing and adaption* will refer to the use of feedback in adaption or modification. For example, we find simple rules govern the behavior of crowds, as we note that agents in these crowds maintain a certain distance from one another and tend to follow others who have already created paths (Moussaid, Helbing, & Theraulaz, 2011).

As I began using complexity theory in my research endeavors, I, like others, applied the term incorrectly. For example, complicated interactions often are referred to as "the complexities" of disabilities, abuse, and substance abuse. In current literature we see articles about the "complexities" of various phenomena (e.g., Mizrahi & Rosenthal, 2001). While these writings provide useful information on multifaceted issues, discussing the interactions of variables or levels of difficulty in resolving a situation, we view complexity differently. Such use of the term "complexity" should not be confused with what Patton (2011) refers to as "complicated." Patton's classification scheme uses three levels; the first, *simple,* includes easy-to-follow instructions that when followed will result in an expected outcome. The second, *complicated,* involves more parts or steps, similar to following a blueprint for building an item with many parts, and that achieves an anticipated result if followed correctly. The third level, *complex,* will be our focus, and centers on the concept of nonlinear dynamics because of the increased uncertainty resulting from all the interconnections affecting our inquiry.

Complexity theory has entered the mainstream media. For example, the *New York Times* often carries stories from researchers at the Santa Fe Institute. One such article talks with the noted physicist Geoffrey West. In this he describes the emergence of cities and the underlying patterns that explain their maintenance and patterns of growth (Lehrer, 2010). In another example, Wikipedia, the online encyclopedia, demonstrates how complexity and the self-organizing behavior of a group of individuals with a keen interest on a specific topic can create a coherent response to share with others. Although followers of certain politicians or other groups may try to rewrite entries in Wikipedia, keepers of site that are important to them will readily correct erroneous information.

Examples of self-organizing are found in the Campbell Collaboration and Cochrane Collaborations as researchers with similar interests collaborate to identify trends in evidence-based practices. Recently developed *in silico* tools, including *new media*, encourage a promising vehicle toward creating social change. Although not identified as such, several popular books advance complexity related ideas. Brooks (2011) in *The Social Animal* reveals the subconscious reasoning we humans make, while Gladwell (2000) in *The Tipping Point* discusses the logic behind the emergence of trends.

COMPLEXITY'S MULTIDISCIPLINARY BACKGROUND

The study of complex systems emerged from several disciplines. Most prominent were influences provided from computer science, theoretical physics, ecology, economics, linguistics, and neuroscience (Lewin, 1999). Computer science provided the computational means to develop inquiry and create the simulations needed to create the multilayered models present in the study of complex systems. Theoretical physics played a key role as quantum mechanics emerged early in the twentieth century as a representation of the patterns found in apparent randomness. Ecology interestingly played a key role in the development of complexity because of its reliance on the study of ecosystems. On this aspect, social work appears to have missed an opportunity to play a prominent role in the field's emergence.

Game theory from the field of economics was an important development in the formation of complexity as a research paradigm. The cooperative and competitive games that agents play, while seeking to maximize their outcomes even though they have incomplete information of the other agent's intentions, were antecedent to developing agent-based modeling. Linguistics likewise played an key role in developing complexity theory because of the need to create an efficient language to express the constructs under study. Creating an efficient language became increasingly important, with algorithms and relational algebra used for the transmission of information. Neuroscience another initial influence, continues to be a prime avenue of investigation, and serves as an essential influence because of its reliance on networks present through the central nervous system. In order to apply a complexity paradigm to social work, we need to shift from a pure hypothesis-testing approach to an increasingly exploratory and nonlinear method. From these six initial influences, we move on to more specific contemporary social work applications in chapter 3.

THEORETICAL FOUNDATIONS

While several mathematical, statistical, and methodological aspects related to complex systems will be discussed later, a few theoretical foundations need to be introduced briefly as they will be useful in understanding this paradigm's development.

Game Theory

In its basic form, game theory follows two distinct types, competitive and leader/follower games. Game theory involves the mathematics of incomplete information, within which agents try to maximize potential outcomes while not knowing all there is to know about their competition. Understanding these games is important, because we live in an environment where resources are limited. Social workers at all levels—whether administrators, clinicians, or evaluators—must compete for these scarce resources. Game theory provides the conceptual framework for maximizing potential payoffs while making decisions with incomplete information about the competition. In many situations, such as developing a new grant proposal or creating an array of services for a broad group of potential clients, these competitive games may lead to cooperation; but the purpose remains to outcompete another individual or group to acquire the resources. Participants in the game develop and implement their strategies to maximize their likelihood of obtaining resources.

For a client, the sought-after resource might be time with direct service providers; for administrators, the goal may be expanded access to a network of interagency contacts that would improve the robustness of the organization; for an executive director, it could involve gaining a competitive advantage against other service providers who are viewed as threats to the organization's survival. For the purposes of complexity, game theory aids in formulating the decision rules of individual agents.

Network Science

This recently developed field seeks to identify common characteristics, algorithms, and methods across the broad range of networks found in physical and social sciences. Foremost, network science examines the interconnections (linkages) prevalent in the diverse range of networks. It involves more than the ubiquitous online social networks or the rigorous field of social network analysis; it entails the study of *network thinking*. Based on the premise that we are interconnected and these interconnections influence our thoughts, behaviors, and actions, network science cuts across many domains.

Applications of networks within organizations focus on the domains of individual agents, tasks performed by individual agents, and resources that are accumulated and used by individual agents. Network thinking and social work practice share values. This line of thinking assists in bridging the resources from micro and macro practice to improve peoples' quality of life (Tracy & Brown, 2011). The section on social network analysis in chapter 4 will deal with this field in greater depth. Networks are all around us (Castells, 2004) and represent the vast interconnectedness of entities. For example, we can see the dynamic capacities of networks when discussing plasticity of the brain. In the brain's circuits, once damage occurs in certain lobes or regions, other areas of the brain will begin to compensate for this. In effect, the brain begins to rewire itself. This example of networks demonstrates the usefulness of redundancy.

As an administrator for a social service organization for two decades, I was often surprised when funding sources sought to eliminate redundancy in their service array. What was referred to as a "duplication of services" could have been seen as a positive event, because it encouraged competition between organizations and provided resiliency in case one organization began to perform below expectations. In effect, resources could be shifted to programs and services providing better outcomes. Other networking examples include neural networks (synapses and dendrites), transportation (public transit and the hub and spoke systems of airlines) and social (who knows who knows whom; online sites). The lack of social networks, conversely, can have negative effects, as noted by

Durkheim (1951) : individuals with fewer people in their networks have a higher likelihood of committing suicide.

General Systems Theory

This well-known antecedent to complexity theory is quite familiar to social workers. The application of general systems theory (GST) becomes apparent when discussing ecosystems (Andreae, 2011). GST aids in understanding the dynamic and interconnected agents present in networks or organizations. Briefly, GST came from the science and engineering fields and built on the concept that simple one-way cause-and-effect patterns can explain phenomena. When applied to social work, GST implies a PIE, but the influence of the person on their environment is not as clear. Within GST systems are dynamic, with the components of the system constantly changing (von Bertalanffy, 1968).

Ecosystems Theory

GST lead to the formulation of the ecological framework, in which we move beyond the systems in the person's sphere, in order to focus on the interconnections of client systems and the larger environment. Therefore, people and their environment reach out and adapt to each other (Bronfenbrenner, 1994; Germain & Gitterman, 1980). Through applying open systems, we more clearly include the external influences affecting human functioning. Similar to complex systems, ecosystems theory is applied at multiple levels (micro, mezzo, exo, and macro levels). At the micro level we look at influences of the persons surrounding environment (e.g., family, school, work). At the mezzo level, the relationships between these environmental influences are better understood. At the exo level, we study the influences that do not directly interact with the individual, but still have influence (e.g., the influence of the parents' workplaces on the children). At the macro level we are concerned with the ideologies and values of society and how these may influence the individual.

Cybernetics

This field concentrates on how feedback informs systems. Such approaches may include learning systems and quality improvement efforts found in most licensed or accredited social service programs. Formally, cybernetics is the study of communication and control (Wiener, 1961). Positive and negative feedback play central roles in the study of cybernetics (when discussing feedback, positive and negative do not imply good and bad). Positive feedback amplifies or expands upon what has occurred within a system. Negative feedback helps to regulate a system by serving as a control mechanism. Examples include mandated programs, such as unemployment insurance to assist in dampening the fluctuations in family income, or the performance measures used in quality improvement systems required by accreditation bodies.

Both positive and negative feedback loops are required for a system to operate smoothly. Stable systems tend to have strong negative feedback. Complex systems in social work tend to be open rather than closed. By this, we mean that external influences, beyond what is in the client's immediate systems, affect individuals within the system. For example, US Supreme Court decisions on least restrictive environments will affect an individual's ability to seek and obtain housing in a community.

Outcome monitoring and quality improvement using cybernetic methods are vital to improving the efficacy and efficiency of social service organizations. Current organizational evaluative and improvement methods that concentrate only on linear aspects, such as outputs of services (e.g., cost per unit of service, number of consumers provided services in a given time period) cannot account for the constantly changing environment in which these organizations operate. In response to this dilemma, complexity models often use temporal and spatial data to better account for social conditions that are contingent upon location and time.

COMPLEXITY RELATED CONCEPTS

The term complex system provides the vehicle by which complexity can be framed in social service situations. It serves as the host for complexity; therefore it is beneficial that the terminology be explained and that the concepts defined, so that they align with the language used in social work. Before moving on to chapter 2, where the components of such complex systems are discussed and serve to frame complexity oriented research and evaluation, several concepts related to complexity can be introduced. It is often through these concepts that complexity occurs and becomes apparent within our environment. These concepts play an essential role in grounding complexity into social work practice.

Sensitivity to Initial Conditions

Many of us are familiar with this concept—also referred to as *the edge of chaos*—through the butterfly effect. Initially proposed by the mathematician and meteorologist Edward Lorenz (1963), this concept arose while he was developing a method to predict weather. To save valuable computer space in the 1960s, he modified his initial data slightly and ran the program from the middle of the initial run. In effect he had reduced his model from six decimal places to three. This slight change resulted in dramatically different outcomes. Metaphorically, a typical example goes like this: the small effect of a butterfly's wings flapping causes a chain of events, which in turn leads to a large-scale weather event at a distant location. This sensitivity to initial conditions is viewed as leading to chaos. The salient point being made is that small changes can have massive unintended consequences, characteristic of chaos theory.

All this leads to realizing that not all is predictable[1]. This can be seen as sensitivity to initial conditions. There are similarities to quantum mechanics, where we may understand the random patterns of electrons around the nucleus of an atom, but we cannot predict the individual paths of the individual electrons.[2] Although the concept of sensitivity to initial conditions appears similar to Heisenberg's Second Law of Thermodynamics, they are fundamentally different. Sensitivity to initial conditions is concerned with determinate, albeit unpredictable, conditions; whereas the Second Law of Thermodynamics is fundamentally indeterminate. In this new scientific paradigm of complexity, disorder means something. What appears to be chaotic behavior can actually be mapped by plotting graphically the calculations of nonlinear mathematics. This involves the use of fractal geometry, as developed by Benoit Mandelbrot, where symmetrical patterns repeat across different scales (Gleick, 1987).

Social work appears particularly suited to applying this concept because both historically and currently, policies, programs, and services often emerge from chaotic social conditions. This was particularly true for developing urban areas in the United States, as they experienced major shifts in available employment in the late nineteenth century. In response to dire conditions in these urban cores, social insurance policies emerged in several individual states—both unemployment insurance and workers' compensation. In a matter of years, these initial efforts from individual states became the framework for federal standards that were applied across the entire country.

A related concept is crowd and anti-crowd theory. This theory involves dichotomous whether-or-not questions (0 representing not, 1 representing yes) that refer to whether an agent chooses participation (Johnson, 2009). This concept will be revisited in chapters 6 and 7, when agent-based modeling is discussed,; it provides the basis for cellular automata. Crowd and anti-crowd theory also involves on/off switches, and indicates whether an agent chooses to participate. Exactly how clients and prospective clients respond and provide feedback can be contingent on scarce resources within the dynamical system. Johnson (2007) further discusses the effects of crowds and anti-crowds. The crowd represents the agents following the emergent behavior, whereas with the anti-crowd, the agents are choosing not to participate in the emergent behavior. Anti-crowds induce a level of chaotic behavior in the population.

Conflict/Cooperation

A colleague has a sign on her desk that reads "BECAUSE NICE MATTERS." What we can summarize is that on occasion, we may have different ideas to solve a problem, and possibly different solutions entirely. However, a healthy and frank discussion leads to informed agents and, therefore, better decisions. We see simple examples of cooperation daily—for example, when traffic narrows by one lane, drivers alternatively allow one car to merge from each lane in successive order. In social work treatment, it may occasionally be better to induce a crisis so that clients can get past a significant issue. In the end, however, after a period of conflict, we need to move toward cooperation. Cooperation may be seen as simple sharing—for example a growing belief in the technology sector envisions information-sharing as a healthy approach to corporate growth, as companies like Google, Twitter, and Facebook compete by cooperating and holding onto two assumptions: innovation involves collaboration, and the expanding market of online products has no limits (Ferenstein, 2011).

As I was about to graduate with my bachelor's degree, my first job in social services involved living with a young adult who had grown up in an institution. My role involved living with him as a roommate, and to assist in his normalization (a concept from the 1970s when persons with disabilities were beginning to be included in their communities). One issue concerned the lack of power this person had over his environment, as I really made a large number of his decisions. The aspects of *conflict and cooperation* emerged. Empowerment in one's environment serves as an indicator of quality of life. In this setting, my roommate had little.

In the 1970s, field experiences and internships for college students for those focused on working with persons with a disability occurred primarily in segregated employment programs, institutions, and day programs. These programs had the stated purpose of assuring that the clients (persons with disabilities) were working and receiving training to develop basic abilities such as adult living skills (ALS). Unlike current approaches, such as supported employment, these settings rarely prepared individuals sufficiently for entry into the job market. Behavior modification techniques—such as intermittent schedules of reinforcement—were popular with many in human services, the thinking being that this could bring about meaningful change for persons with disabilities. These rigid approaches have evolved during the intervening three decades so persons with disabilities are encouraged to be participating members in their communities and to make their own decisions.[3]

Diverse Perspectives

Intuitively, social workers know the value of diversity, however, how can these benefits be quantified? Beyond the obvious advantages of including persons with diverse ethnic backgrounds, there lies the logic for valuing individual differences. Because of its adaptive nature, complexity provides an investigative structure within and across both qualitative and quantitative methods. In addition to the obvious links to the metaphorical aspects of complexity in a qualitative sense and the highly computational aspects involved in quantitative methods, complexity and its related components provide the mixed-model researcher a model of diversity that similarly provides implications for inquiry using diverse methods. In academia, our research foci may become very narrow. We benefit by using interdisciplinary approaches to avoid this when it becomes problematic. For example, over the past few years I have become interested in public transit issues for persons with disabilities; however, a large deal of overlap with that topic occurs when addressing issues of older adults.

An overall approach to problem solving uses two steps: first an encoding of the problem (perspective), and second, ways to manipulate the solution (heuristics). From these conditions, people can use a toolbox of diverse abilities and knowledge to arrive at the best solution. Diverse perspectives and heuristics on the individual and group level will lead to a larger set of possible solutions for the group. Essential to this idea is the understanding that people may disagree about an outcome; diversity creates group assets that allow for solving and making predictions of difficult phenomena (Page, 2007, 2011).

Diverse Heuristics for Problem Solving

In qualitative research, we see the concepts of networks and complexity when we develop a snowball sample to inquire into difficult-to-reach populations (Newman, 2010). By seeking the knowledge of a diverse group of individuals through this snowball effect, we are able to begin using the wisdom of crowds to obtain a range of ideas and opinions.

Diverse perspectives lead to innovation and parallels with the emerging method of developmental evaluation. This has implications to mixed methods research, given our desire to blend appropriate methodologies when conducting social inquiry. We learn to respect and appreciate the robustness of the group in which the members possess diverse backgrounds and experiences. When discussing diverse perspectives, we learn that these lead to a coalescing of information rather than an unmanageable tangle of thoughts. Diversity benefits are derived from applications for problem solving, aggregating information, and forecasting outcomes based on the perspectives and wisdom of individuals in crowds.

Niche Construction

Adapted from ecology, this concept provides a useful construct for developing resilience and robustness among individuals, families, and groups seeking social services. Niche construction aids in understanding the barriers that individuals and groups encounter as they strive to become fully included in their environments. Especially in an ecosystems approach, this concept assists in determining how some clients receiving services are successful while others are not. This concept's usefulness lies in assessing how agents (clients) may alter their environment by using feedback to improve their likelihood for success and improving their quality of life. More recently, this appears to be a promising construct for inquiry about how social service clients enter transitional phases, and this plays an important role as services to persons with disabilities increasingly become oriented toward full inclusion (Flack, Girvan, de Waal, & Krakauer, 2006).

Robustness and Resiliency

As introduced by Holling (1973), two beliefs underpin resilience theory. The first states that people and nature are strongly interconnected and therefore may be viewed as a single system; the second is that this single system responds to constant changes in the environment by using multiple feedback loops in a nonlinear manner (Folke, 2010). Consistent with social work and complexity theory, robustness can be engineered, facilitated, and built into systems (Bednar, 2009). Robustness conceptually applies across both macro and micro practice in social work. At the macro level, governmental policies and supports may sustain a family through essential services such as income maintenance and health care. At the micro level, social work interventions attempt to make individuals and families more resilient to threats, so that when they occur (e.g., unemployment), the family unit maintains a basic level of service. The discussion on social networks will further support the linkages of micro and macro level social work practice.

Self-Similarity

In mathematical terms, self-similarity refers to an object that is exactly or closely similar to a part of itself. These geometric shapes, called fractals, have a fine structure at every scale, and exhibit self-similarity at each of these scales. Fractals provide a useful means to link iteration with dynamic processes. For example, in generalist social work education, several methods are taught which can be generalized across settings and populations. Developing goals and objectives can be applied to clinical settings and to designing a program evaluation. While applied in diverse situations, essentially the same skills are displayed. Generalist social work practice appears based on the idea of self-similarity, as the skills learned can be applied across multiple settings and at different scales.

Scalability

In the simplest sense, scalability refers to economies of scale. For example, when an intervention is developed and formalized for replication, the initial cost of development has already been borne by the developers, and therefore each successive use of the materials decreases. Commonly, scalability refers to a system or network's ability to accommodate growth capacity without harming the system or network. As social service organizations seek to identify approaches that will produce more units of service with limited resources, continued attempts to become more efficient arise.

Wisdom of Crowds

This concept refers to the value that diverse perspectives and diverse heuristics provide when applied to problem solving (Alexander, 2009; Surowiecki, 2004). Four characteristics are needed to reap the benefits of wisdom of crowds: diverse opinions amongst the agents present; independent opinions within these diverse agents; the ability of individuals in the crowd to draw upon their local or self-developed knowledge and experience; and a process to aggregate individual opinions, knowledge, or experience into a collective decision.

SOCIAL SERVICES AND COMPLEXITY

Social workers can use complexity to understand what attracts agents (clients) to interventions, and then to see how these agents self-organize in order to establish an emergent behavior. Complexity provides a promising structure for inquiry within and across both qualitative and quantitative methods. Applying it to direct services poses greater obstacles given the inconsistent use and availability of reliable longitudinal and location data within human service organizations. When applied in the social service field to analyze social systems and processes on micro and macro levels, complexity may include computational methods, pattern recognition, and modeling approaches that emphasize simulations in order to understand emerging issues (Wheatley, 1999).

Social service organizations are dynamic as they continually improve and respond to changing environmental conditions. They benefit by becoming learning organizations through applying Peter Senge's five disciplines of learning organizations (2006). Organizations can develop group problem-solving abilities that are effective in response to changing environmental conditions. Applying the five disciplines (personal mastery, developing mental models for conceptualizing, building a shared vision, encouraging team learning, and facilitating systems thinking to integrate these concepts) aids personnel in developing the capacity to aspire, reflect, and understand the complex nature of their organization's environment.

Social work managers and planners typically live in a quantitative world, whereas practitioners are in a qualitative world. Complexity serves as a vehicle for resolving the barriers between the two by having both become enabling researchers (Padgett, 2004). Complexity provides a promising alternative approach because it deals with issues such as (1) inclusion of the researcher, (2) broadening the historic and political context, and (3) issues of prediction (Agar, 1999). Potential applications for social work cover a broad scope ranging from historical analyses to understanding emerging social phenomena, to applying trajectory growth curves in clinical trials.

Contemporary social work research and evaluation models often encourage using mixed-methods that apply both qualitative and quantitative approaches when examining the effects of social programs (Creswell, 2003). The problem remains that these mixed-models use methods separately; therefore, they lack integration between the qualitative and quantitative data. The application of complexity theory to social work research and evaluation provides a solution to this dissonance by integrating both qualitatively based process information and quantitatively based outcome measures. When applied correctly, complexity suggests a framework that is both iterative and nonreductionist.

Complex systems and contemporary social service practice share several attributes, including (1) decisions should come from the client level or grassroots level, (2) attractors are instrumental in clients maintaining interest and completing interventions, (3) boundaries, (4) client and organizational feedback are vital to improving outcomes, and (5) self-organization leads to an emergent behavior.

"The Holy Grail of Complexity in Science," observed Johnson (2009), "is to understand, forecast and control such emergent phenomena—in particular, potentially catastrophic crowd-like effects such as market crashes, traffic jams, epidemics, illnesses such as cancer, human conflicts, and environmental change..

Although social work issues are not the focus in Johnson's quote, they are at least mentioned tangentially. Certain phenomena, such as the evolution of technology, can take on their own life (Kelly, 2010). Paramount to this is that complex systems are a bottom–up approach, whereby the decisions of individuals and their families lead to a collective or emergent group behavior.

The study of complexity may be relatively recent; however, the underlying tenets have historical precedent. Several prominent social scientists have recognized the value of inquiry based on individual decisions and the role of simple rules in making decisions. Before the formalization of complexity theory, Adam Smith, the father of modern economics two centuries ago noted:

> Every individual naturally inclines to employ his capital in the manner in which it is likely to afford the greatest support to domestic industry, and to give revenue and employment to the greatest number of people of his own country (invisible hand).

As we can see, this notion of the invisible hand represents a complex phenomenon, because a force is guiding decisions.

Given the variety of social program evaluation techniques, it's little wonder that researchers and evaluators in the field occasionally encounter confusion when determining their program's effectiveness. This chapter provides a structure for framing evaluation efforts, and introduces the lexicon of complex systems and CAS to research and evaluation efforts. The discussion for developing this framework given CAS's dynamic ability can include various data types, including primary and secondary, historical and current, temporal and spatial, to name a few.

Most complex systems are adaptive and seek to identify an underlying order in what initially appears as chaotic or disorderly phenomenon. This theoretical approach has potential applications in consumer and organizational decision making, planning, and outcomes management. It helps us understand the possible emergent behaviors that arise when diverse agents are in specific geographic and resource contexts. It may also include inquiry into how behavior adapts to contextual features, particularly the spatial properties and the relative availability of desired resources within those locales.

Complexity arises from the interactions of competitive and cooperative tendencies of agents. Such systems are in a continual state of dynamic equilibrium, and they navigate between being in rigid order and in chaos. These systems operate according to a set of simple rules, yet patterns emerge from these simple interactions without a predetermined template (Mankiewicz, 2001). Contemporary social service practice shares several attributes found in complex systems theory. These attributes include the following.

- Decisions come from the client level or grassroots level
- Attractors and self-organization are instrumental in clients maintaining interest and completing interventions
- Limits, laws, and rules set boundaries
- Client and organizational feedback are vital to improving outcomes
- The above components lead to an emergent behavior.

In addition to these attributes found in the components of a complex system, several issues include using conflict to develop cooperation (Axelrod, 1984); having threats to a social network improve that network's robustness and resiliency; and using the wisdom of crowds, represented by diverse characteristics of group members for the purpose of improving decision making (Page, 2007; Surowiecki, 2004).

Complexity theory can be applied to a broad range of activities. Students and organizers may be familiar with the conflict-oriented approach forwarded in Saul Alinsky's *Rules for Radicals* (1971), one example of complex theory applicable to working with communities. In contemporary practice, however, we are more likely to follow a cooperative technique such as community building or consensus organizing. as proposed by Eichler (2007), or seek to alleviate oppression and facilitate empowerment (Homan, 2011). We can link the application of resilience at multiple systems levels in service delivery (Greene, 2007) to the complexity concept of robustness. Through shared decision making (Maple, 1977) and person-centered planning strategies, social workers appreciate the partnerships created through using the diverse perspectives and heuristics in planning interventions, as explained in the examples in chapter 5.

LINKING THESE CONCEPTS TO SOCIAL WORK

Recently, I taught a class for the first time on empowering communities for change. In prior research and evaluation classes that I've taught, the materials were oriented to assessing the performance of social service organizations and designed to conduct interventions where clients can choose participation through completion, participation before program completion, or nonparticipation. Evaluation of these interventions, however, relied typically on reductionist approaches that investigate the overall achievement of program objectives rather than the collective behavior of individuals or families.

The blending of materials for course work—a process of combining and winnowing—took on a new shape as the concept of organizing became fresh to me again. As I began preparing course materials and reviewed Eichler's (2007) text on Consensus Organizing, I better understood how complexity pervades and, therefore, how it provides a unique paradigm for framing inquiry. In Eicher's initial chapter, four approaches to community organizing are proposed: conflict organizing, women-centered organizing, community-building organizing, and consensus organizing. Using these four approaches, we can gain a stronger initial understanding of complex systems.

Conflict organizing is the approach least consistent with complexity theory. It uses anger and blame on a defined individual or group. The objective of this approach is to place pressure on the identified person or group to create a concession or change. While some cooperation may emerge out of the conflict, this approach most resembles gaining power, not sharing it in a cooperative manner. This would be contrary to a complexity theory perspective.

Contrary to a conflict organizing approach, women-centered organizing is a power-sharing approach where community participants and the organizer are committed to creating balanced power relationships through democratic practices of shared leadership, decision making, and responsibility for implementing the decisions. From this initial description, we begin to see how this approach more closely resembles a complex system because of the greater likelihood that the decisions, the implementation of the decisions, and the self-organizing behavior will come from the grassroots.

In social work, the community-building approach uses local stakeholders to form collaborations that strengthen their capacity to solve problems. This approach increasingly resembles complexity theory, as the notion of collaboration and less conflict become the means for creating social change. The fourth approach, consensus organizing, links the self-interest of the community to the self-interests of others in order to achieve a shared goal. This approach most resembles the positive outcomes we would expect to achieve. Consensus organizing can be used to create interest and to get people involved who may have diverse experiences and problem-solving skills. In effect, within a complexity outlook, community building and consensus organizing become the most consistent approaches because they use the strengths of the community members as strengths upon which the community can be developed.

Aspects of community organizing are found in the writings of Mondros and Wilson (1994) and Freire (1994). Mondros and Wilson stress the model of grassroots organizing that addresses the differences that people in power and people who are marginalized have. The goal is for regular citizens who have been marginalized, to work collaboratively and self-organize into a powerful group to affect change with those in power who often are resistant to change.

Freire (1994) assumed a social change approach that was more focused on consciousness-raising and education. He was critical of a *banking education* view—which assumed that knowledge is a possession that teachers give to students—and of education that traditionally occurs where the learners must listen and obey. He forwarded a process called *problematizing education* in which organizing becomes a dialogic process that recognizes power awareness, critical literacy, desocialization, and self-organization (Pyles, 2009). As we will see, Freire's approach aligns well with participatory action research so that agents of change become educated and can influence others at the grassroots.

As we apply complexity to social service organizations and community practice, we understand that the persons, or other units of analysis, are the agents, and these entities are located at the grassroots. The initial conditions that these agents possess can be identified and expressed simply through descriptive statistics. These agents are the intended audiences, and they determine whether these agents do in fact have the position to make decisions. If they do, then the analysis begins to check whether there is an attraction, or if self-organizing behavior occurs. This self-organizing behavior may be exhibited as a form of autocorrelation, and may be represented by either spatial or temporal methods. If so, then we can inquire as to why these agents are seeking services, and if so, what maintains their interest in continuing to receive services, and finally what leads these individuals to complete services. Finally, the simple rules, or heuristics, of the collective behavior can be identified. Using a complexity approach, social service inquiry seeks the identification of these simple rules.

As we delve into this research paradigm, it is valuable to realize that the study of complexity has interdisciplinary influences including linguistics, cognitive neuroscience, computer science, theoretical physics, and ecology. Throughout this book, these influences will be addressed. With the advent of immediate communications, large datasets, computational power, and electronic social networking, we are well positioned to use these interdisciplinary influences to affect social change.

This begins in chapter 2 where the components of complex systems are described in order to provide the basis for developing research oriented to complexity theory. Chapter 3 reviews traditional and current research methods that may be applicable to use collaboratively with a complexity approach; the methods discussed all reflect a bottom–up approach that includes the diverse perspectives of participants. Chapter 4 reviews mathematical and theoretical underpinnings for complexity theory and suggests the appropriate inferential statistical methods to use in concert with agent-based models. Chapter 5 discusses four applications of complexity theory in social work research and evaluation, where the concepts introduced in this chapter are discussed in greater detail. These discussions form the basis for developing agent-based models in chapters 6 and 7. As you may notice when reading chapters 6 and 7, agent-based modeling primarily will serve as a descriptive method with limited inferential statistics, similar to social network analysis. Chapter 7 provides information on developing models that build upon traditional social work research methods. In chapter 8, future applications of complexity theory are discussed through developing a research agenda for this emerging paradigm in social work.

SUMMARY

In this first chapter, several of the antecedents leading to the development of complexity as a scientific paradigm were discussed and related concepts of complexity were introduced. These concepts lay the groundwork for applying complexity in social service situations. In chapter 2, the components comprising a complex system are introduced to provide a framework for using complexity metaphorically. You will begin to identify these components within a social service environment. This step will be essential as we move toward applying agent-based modeling to simulate and generate social work related issues.

EXERCISES

1. It is often difficult to anticipate how minor modifications can produce chaotic behavior within an organization. Based on your past social work experiences within an organization, describe how one small change in a service delivery resulted in large unintended consequences.
2. Go to the Santa Fe Institute website (http://www.santafe.edu). Review the diverse topics addressed and discuss how social work fits with two or more of their content areas. Then propose an initial research agenda for yourself that incorporates complexity related concepts.
3. The wisdom of crowds relates directly to using diverse perspectives and heuristics of individuals in problem solving. Ask each person in your class to provide an estimate of a selected social service phenomenon. This may include an estimate of the volume of services provided by an organization, or the average length-of-stay for persons receiving interventions from an organization.
4. Most readers of this book will have already developed a flowchart to represent how a system operates. Flowcharting likewise provides a useful tool for visualizing the process involved in typical social service delivery. Using an organizational process with which you are familiar (e.g., intake process), develop a flowchart that represents the current system. Create a second flowchart that represents a simplified version of the current process.

2

Framing Social Services as Complex Systems

Building on theory, history, and concepts, this chapter introduces the components of complex systems. Knowing what defines a complex system sets the course for the remainder of this book. Grasping an understanding of these components provides an essential link for properly identifying variables and related data sources. This chapter concludes with these concepts being applied to an environment that provides services for persons with intellectual disabilities.

Learning objectives for chapter 2 include

- an understanding of how social service interventions can be framed as complex systems;
- an ability to analyze a social-service-based complex system and deconstruct it into its components.

Complex systems contain several components. Applying complexity to social work begins by defining these components. This requires that we first deconstruct social service interventions into the components of complex systems theory. These components include being agent-based, having a choice of options, having defined boundaries, occurring within an organization, allowing for self-organization, using feedback, and producing an emergent behavior (Morowitz, 2002). Within the complexity paradigm, we move beyond the basic linear approaches that serve as the premises of developing and evaluating social service programs. We become increasingly interested in the interconnections between individuals, families, and communities, and how these linkages relate to their environment.

In this chapter we build upon the basic components inherent to social service organizations, including mission statements, goals, and objectives. While this linear thinking provides a good foundation for creating responsive social programs, with a complexity theory approach we view social service delivery as a system in which we are able to identify the interconnectedness and interactions. We seek to understand how clients function and how organizations attempt to alleviate client concerns by working cooperatively with them.

DECONSTRUCTING THE COMPLEX INTO COMPONENTS

It is somewhat ironic that applying the complexity paradigm to social work begins with deconstructing a complex system into its component parts. This is necessary because we seek to understand interactions derived from these components and the agents present in the system. To begin, Figure 2.1 provides an overview of the interaction of components typically found in a complex system. It is through these components, especially the self-organizing and feedback elements, that a complex system arises and maintains itself. The individual components are described below.

AGENT-BASED

Complex systems are built with individual units (agents). Being agent-based broadly means defining our unit of measure as the agent. The agent can be an individual, family, group, or community. It is the interactions, the emerging networks of relationships, and the collective emergent behavior resulting from interactions of these agents in their communities and other situations that is of interest to us. Understanding that complexity assumes a bottom–up as opposed to a top–down approach is essential. It is the

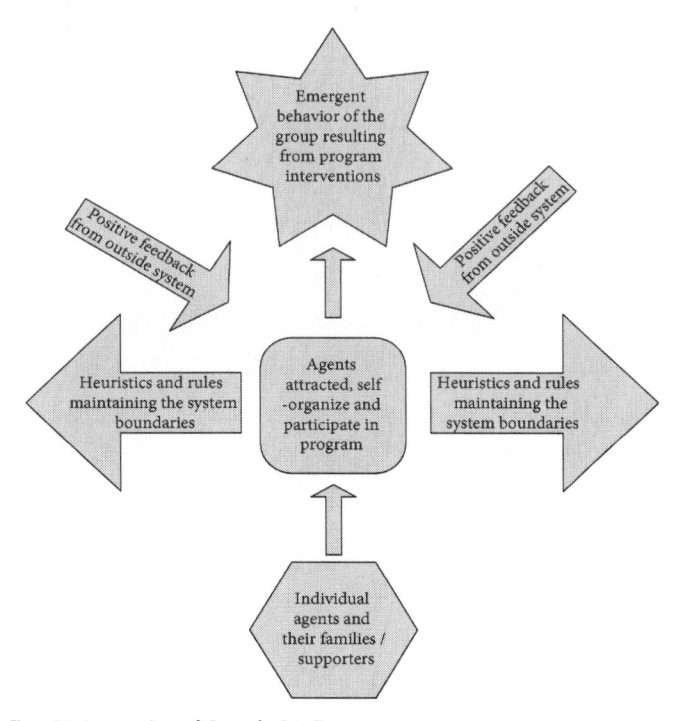

Figure 2.1 Interaction of Complexity Components.

complexity resulting from these interactions that provides the wealth of information that keeps the approach from being reductionist.

SENSITIVITY TO INITIAL CONDITIONS

This component parallels well with the client, group, or grassroot organizational levels in social work. Complexity modeling begins with the agent, and in social work this initial unit of analysis likely remains at the client, family, group, or community level. A key aspect is determining how these agents function, form relationships with similar agents, make decisions, and eventually self-organize. While impacts may come from supervisory influences and people or entities in higher-ranking positions, within complexity it is at this client level that agents organize. An example of initial conditions within social work practice may be found in Wolf-Branigin, Schuyler, & White (2007), which indicated that adolescents who had a disability improved their likelihood for employment success if they received early (age 13) intervention services to improve their attitude toward work and quality of life. These life skills and positive attitudes toward future employment provided the requisite skills, knowledge, and abilities to become self-sufficient and reduce their use of Supplemental Security Income (SSI) as their sole income when they became adults.

ATTRACTION AND SELF-ORGANIZATION

These related components are most easily viewed as the magnet (variable) that draws people together; identifies what attracts clients/agents; and pinpoints what maintains their involvement in a group, initiative, or other organized structure (Kaufmann, 1995). Adaptation or self-organization aspects include agents deciding to continue participation, and the formulation of interconnected natural and mutual supports among themselves in order to acquire quality-of-life improvements and career options. For example, when identifying what single factor explained clients continuing their involvement in a faith-based substance abuse treatment program, Wolf-Branigin and Duke (2007) identified involvement in spiritual activities as the key element to remaining active and completing a treatment program. The organization provides a location or identity where agents interact and share information. When applied to social work, possible examples of organizations include self-help groups, behavioral or physical health providers, educational settings, and services to children and families. The organization refers to the system under which all of these activities occur.

HETEROGENEITY

This component of complex systems refers to the array of options within the agent's ecosystem from which individual agents choose. Environments in which agents have limited choices reduce the utility of a complexity approach. Complexity advances the concept of ecosystems by having as the researcher's goal to understand the exigencies that account for more than simple cause-and-effect explanations in behavior (Bolland & Atherton, 1999). Complexity concerns itself with viewing the complete set of variables affecting client behaviors (Agar, 1999; Halmi, 2003). The heterogeneous organizing component becomes the different program options from which the adolescents and their families choose. This may include the agents' decision to remain active in an employment readiness program, or to seek service elsewhere, or not to continue with any service. We can see this when clients are provided options. Heterogeneity has occurred in services to persons with intellectual or developmental disabilities as these services moved from being institution-based to community-based, and now, in many regions, to individualized planning and budgeting.

ITERATIVE PROCESSES

Complex systems are not static; they have dynamic tendencies that continually evolve and use feedback to inform themselves. These dynamic tendencies include the continually changing environment in which the agents function. Limitations may occur when observing dynamic organizational behaviors. While exploratory approaches support social work's person-in-environment (PIE) paradigm (Padgett, 2004), social work researchers and evaluators need to view the dynamic and continually evolving needs from the client's perspective or from complexity's agent-based. If something is complex, it is relatively unstructured and dynamic (Casti & DePauli, 2000). Examples of dynamic tendencies include adolescents with disabilities acquiring transitioning skills from childhood to adulthood; persons who abuse substances reconnecting with family members; or immigrant populations acculturating as they strive toward becoming citizens of their communities. The key feature of iterative processes is that the output from one phase is used as input for the succeeding phase. These iterations provide feedback for improving the system.

BOUNDARIES

In social service delivery and inquiry, boundaries provide the simple rules or limits that govern the agents' behaviors, decisions, or preferences. These boundaries may also represent the heuristics (problem-solving skills) that contribute to a collective nonlinear emergent behavior. Within social work environments, feedback may result in maintaining current boundaries, or creating new ones through a process where program staff use the strengths, needs, abilities, and preferences of their clients to expand or contract expectations and situations. These changes in boundaries may occur because the organization provides an array of services that reflect the clients' preferences and abilities.

Boundaries may be determined from legislation, court decisions, or administrative rules supporting policies, funding, or incentives. Boundaries play an essential role in understanding and developing a complex adaptive systems (CAS) approach to social program evaluation. For example, Critical Systems Heuristics (Reynolds, 2006; Ulrich, 1996) aids in setting the limits of the evaluation. Boundaries set the limits, define the evaluation's intended audience, and determine the boundaries agents follow that lead to an emergent behavior.

ADAPTATION

This component refers to an organization's ability to respond to the emerging preferences chosen by agents within the organizations (Strunk, Friedlmayer, & Brousek, 2003). For example, needs assessment using spatial (location) data within a complexity approach has included the planning and observation of emergent behavior related to persons with developmental disabilities, physical disabilities, and housing patterns for persons with low-to moderate incomes (Wolf-Branigin, LeRoy, & Miller 2001). Advances in computing power and ease of use with software packages encourage new methods of simulating social work phenomena. Occurrences of clusters, also known as hotspots, can further represent self-organization as it relates to both temporal and spatial autocorrelation and variability by exploring both positive and negative organizational feedback mechanisms.

DYNAMIC USE OF FEEDBACK

Most commonly associated with the second wave of systems thought (cybernetics), this component explains how systems inform themselves in order to improve decision-making. Positive feedback involves an organization's ability to use information outside of its system, and continues until reaching its useful limits. The terms positive and negative feedback do not imply "good" or "bad" but rather amplification and control, respectively. For example, negative feedback often represents an organization's monitoring or quality assurance process to ensure stable, yet continually improving, operations of a social service organization. To understand the application of this component to complexity theory, envision the push–pull forces that organizations encounter as clients internalize the impact of the interventions provided, and how program planners use negative and positive feedback in their decisions for future programming.

Quality improvement and outcome monitoring methods, vital to improving the efficacy and efficiency of social services, create feedback for both clients and the organization (Institute of Medicine of the National Academies, 2006). Feedback includes agents (clients) sharing information, identifying additional resources, and encouraging the other adolescents to remain active and participate in program activities. Recent developments in personnel evaluation use an approach where workers evaluate their supervisors. Rather than reporting their opinions (feedback) to their supervisors directly, they instead report to the supervisor's supervisor.

EMERGENT BEHAVIOR

Nonlinear dynamics, a key aspect of complexity theory, involves understanding the underlying order of phenomena appearing to lack any pattern or trend. Emergent behavior or emergence in systems results from the interactions of agents. Nonlinearity arose from chaos theory, which states that small initial changes can produce very large and unexpected outcomes. The cause may be disproportionate to the effect. The term "sensitivity to initial conditions" reflects nonlinearity.

Emergence is neither guided by an identified leader, nor dissected into interactions. Instead, emergence is used to identify patterns. In social service applications, nonlinearity includes the chaotic, dynamic, and iterative process of clients and their eventual choices (Waldrop, 1992). On a larger organizational scale, this may include the maintenance of an organization or system improvement, or given the vast diversity of consumers receiving services from an organization, their demographic and functional characteristics, and the services provided (Rhee, 2000). Whether applied on the client or organizational level, nonlinearity attempts to locate or recognize a patterned or emergent behavior. Emergence represents the pattern arising from the self-organizing behavior of agents. Agents may initially act independently, but as their interests cross, interact, and interconnect, new patterns develop. These are the emergent behaviors (Patton, 2011). Emergence, for the purpose of social work research and program evaluation, represents the outcomes resulting from the participation of clients. Emergent behavior can be represented by various temporal and spatial autocorrelation indices. Emergence, for example, can represent the housing patterns of individuals who received support coordination from a social service organization that was created to assist individuals with disabilities in their move from institutions to becoming citizens in their local communities. The emergent phenomenon is the outcome we try to quantify.

BUILDING UPON TRADITIONAL RESEARCH METHODS

Integrating a mixed-model decision-making approach applies both qualitative process information and quantitative outcome measures. This suggests an additional benefit for applying complexity theory to human service organizations. These organizations need to make and justify decisions based on small samples and limited information. Administrators availing themselves of a range of qualitative (non-numeric) and quantitative (numeric) data may use current information. This advantage becomes readily apparent in the complexity of data gathered as too frequently it cannot be coded or is otherwise unusable.

Understanding the practice applications provides a basis for integration into a graduate level social work curriculum, including human behavior and the social environment, policy and social justice, and research and evaluation methods. As outcome and quality enhancement methods remain vital for improving the efficacy and efficiency of human services organizations, these methods alone are unable to account for the constantly changing environment in which these organizations operate. The proposal's merits include providing a model *emergence framework* that accounts for a greater use of agent-based information and modeling within a consumer self-determination paradigm.

Social work researchers increasingly use advanced statistical techniques (e.g., hierarchal linear modeling and discriminant analysis); however, these methods still lack the sensitivity to identify emergent consumer self-organizing behaviors. This remains especially true in determining needs of at-risk populations. Broader impacts from the proposed activities expand on current human service research approaches that focus on experimental and quasi-experimental methods. These approaches rely on findings developed by various behavioral, social, and economic disciplines that developed interventions at the micro, mezzo, and macro levels. Focusing on pattern recognition and emergence in evolving human services that support inclusion, self-determination, and consumer empowerment, aids decision makers in their plans for the emerging strengths, preferences, and needs of their consumers.

Social service decision makers often use either cross-sectional or dated information (e.g., U.S. decennial census). To address this problem, we need to provide decision makers with tools to implement an appropriate and rigorous time-sensitive pattern-identification approach by increasing their abilities to identify emerging clusters. Social service organizations applying complex systems theory, as represented by the emergence of spatial relationships (spatial dependencies), demonstrate the ability to improve outcomes resulting from their interventions. Social service organizations improve their decision-making abilities even when given small samples. To facilitate innovation and organizational change, one direction for research aims toward improving upon this knowledge and determining appropriate applications for its use by social service organizations. Such approaches cut across disciplines.

Let's look at some examples. First a social service organization that created housing opportunities for persons with developmental disabilities needs to continually locate and develop appropriate housing and support services. The second application, a rural transportation system, applied a bottom–up or grassroots approach when planning for growing demand for services by designing a needs assessment based on current bus drivers and their customers.

The proposed research applies these methods within a complex systems approach to identify emergent underlying structures for various at-risk populations by using spatial dependencies and autocorrelation. In these applications, spatial dependencies (clusters) indicate that location does provide valuable information on future human service programming. Products resulting from executing the proposed basic research activities include implementation and analysis of the procedures in four human service applications, procedures and documentation for replication of methods in other situations, coding for use in such environments, and a final report documenting the salient issues and findings resulting from the efforts.

Describing complexity involves identifying specific aspects or components typical within social service organizations. These characteristics include knowledge of how the agent (for our purposes, the client receiving services) self-organizes, how attractors operate in order to encourage or facilitate this self-organizing (influences or predictor variables leading to clustering), and how phenomenon functions in a nonlinear manner so that numerous influences are accounted for in opposition to a simple cause and effect. Within the complexity paradigm proposed in this project, spatial data serves as an extension of time series data (Hudson, 2004). This framework provides for the development of spatial methods to forecast and quantify social work phenomena within often apparently chaotic environments.

To begin, we define a complex system with the components of being agent-based, heterogeneous, self-organizing, dynamic, able to provide and use feedback, existing within an organization, and being able to produce an emergent behavior. Sufficiently applying complexity theory to social services involves knowledge of these components that represent these characteristics. This approach appears consistent with the paradigm of *new science*, where the focus centers on the whole system and its interconnectedness, not individual components of the system (Wheatley, 1999). Figure 2.2 presents two examples of applying complexity theory components to two human service interventions. The first is a housing program that serves persons with disabilities who have the opportunity to choose housing options based on their preferences and available locations. The second example reflects transportation services for persons with disabilities, where these riders plan to go, and options for going to their destinations.

Using feedback, both negative and positive, focuses on the proposal's decision-making issues. To understand the application, it becomes useful

Characteristic	Application of Component
Agent-based: Housing organization Transportation service	Persons with a disability Persons who intend to use transit service
Heterogeneity: Housing organization Transportation service	Variety of housing preference Different desired destinations
Dynamic: Housing organization Transportation service	Choice on where to live Desire to move from current location
Feedback: Housing organization Transportation service	Whether location is reasonable Whether rider uses service in the future
Organization: Housing organization Transportation service	Supports coordination organization Regional transit system
Emergent behavior: Housing organization Transportation service	Dispersion of housing pattern Changes in routes to meet riders' preferences

Figure 2.2 Complex Systems Components Applied to Services for Persons with Disabilities.

to realize that push–pull forces operate within organizations. Feedback is found as clients become involved in interventions and internalize the materials or learning provided to them. Organizational planners use both negative and positive feedback in their decisions for future programming. Positive feedback includes an organization's ability to use information outside its system. Positive feedback escalates and continues until bounded. Negative feedback keeps an organization in equilibrium (Proehl, 2001) and is found in the quality assurance, performance improvement, or other management systems designed to inform the decision makers.

The related concept of entropy reflects an organizations inability to confront the loss of energy, often resulting from limited external information (positive feedback) fed back into the decision-making process.

This represents the inability to use information for assuring continued growth and improvement and potential synergies with external organizations, and typically functions in an open system (Shafritz & Ott, 1987; Johnson, 2002). Investigating the decision-making influences used to establish benchmarks within a complex systems approach creates a framework for understanding the significance of evolving combinations of exigencies. Negative feedback, information generated internally in a closed system, uses this information for continual improvement.

Frequently programs and the services provided within them self-perpetuate and are concerned with their own survival. In these instances, workers within these programs may only be looking at the existing services and programs in order to maintain the status quo. Such behavior discourages experimentation and possible new solutions, especially as applied to the combining and winnowing nature that innovative programs exhibit. Combining and winnowing is a useful approach to refine a social work issue, marked by a continual process of obtaining new information through creating potential synergies and then editing for the sake of reducing complications. For example, when working on grant applications, initially several ideas may arise through brainstorming, but as we look at the available resources to conduct the project, the realization arises that not all of the activities are doable. Therefore, this process of combining ideas (looking for synergies) and winnowing (editing expectations) keeps the proposal within reasonable expectations.

Factors influencing what becomes a well-defined social need constantly change. For example, standards of living have improved so that Americans now consider a home without plumbing substandard, whereas a century ago this would not be true. A complex system framework when applied to social policy issues attempts to provide a schema where the continually evolving socio-political concerns, shifting public attitudes, and availability of highly advanced resources and technology contribute to decisions made by planners and administrators of human services. It is an iterative and dynamic process. It produces an emergent or group behavior based on the individual influences from all stakeholders, whether they are clients, staff, community members, or board members.

Assessments of community needs and resources are conducted for one of three reasons: (1) the key stakeholders have to determine whether there is a need for action; (2), a need to design or direct an already contemplated action; or (3), to confirm what is already known about a need, but justification for a decided action requires support. Determining the need for action relates to the complexity component of self-organizing behavior, because if a sufficient number of individuals identify an emergent need, then a tipping point to take action may be achieved. The need to redesign or direct an already contemplated action involves the feedback component and the iterative process of organizational improvement. The final reason, to justify a decided upon action, relates to emergent behavior of the group and the choice to seek to sustain.

Kettner, Moroney, and Martin (2013) describe four types of needs—normative, perceived, expressed, and relative. Normative implies the existence of a standard or criterion. Need is established by custom, authority, or a consensus within a society. Using normative need allows program planners to generate objectives. This approach uses existing information, often expressed as ratios. Determining who is in need involves the concept of "at-risk" and remains fundamental to social service needs assessment. This may be used to channel resources to high-risk areas and populations by setting standards and developing a methodology for counting. Although social service research increasingly applies statistical methods, such as hierarchical linear modeling and factor analysis, to human services to locate nested phenomenon or identify underlying structures, these approaches also rely on static cross-sectional information rather than dynamic time series information that better accounts for emerging trends.

A factor in determining need within at-risk populations is that services for individuals in the past two decades have become increasingly decentralized. As services became community-based and more inclusive within the general population, persons receiving services have increasingly been able to select services based on their preferences and strengths. Applications of self-organizing within a complexity paradigm improve an organization's ability to respond to these emerging preferences (Strunk, Friedlmayer, & Brousek, 2003).

Despite complexity theory not having achieved paradigm status within social service research as defined by Kuhn (1962), the past decade has seen an increase in scholarly articles discussing and applying complexity theory (Bolland & Atherton, 1999; Hudson, 2000, 2004; Trevillon, 2000). Recent publications have enhanced this growing interest and the related area of developmental evaluation (Williams & Imam, 2006;

Westley, Zimmerman, & Patton, 2006). Traditional social work research methods focus on group comparisons, whereas exploratory methods involving correlation and regression attempt to identify linear relationships. Integrating diverse research and evaluative methodologies based on linear relationships and group comparison approaches into a coherent evaluative strategy, however, requires that the methodology be sensitive to time and location.

SUMMARY

This chapter defined the components of a complex system and encouraged the reader to apply these components in a metaphorical sense in order to define a complex system. Understanding how these components interact and then lead to an emergent behavior is essential to creating the agent-based models discussed in later chapters. Readers should learn to distinguish between complex systems, in which complexity may be found through interactions of agents, and CAS, in which the complex system itself also adapts to the environment. Before moving forward to a review of the various statistical approaches used to study complexity, as well as the settings in which complexity may be found and an approach to building agent-based models, we will review in chapter 3 several methodological approaches used in identifying and applying complexity within social service research and evaluation.

Exercises

1. Most of you have completed some social policy coursework. Based on your knowledge of how the Supreme Court of the United States (SCOTUS) operates, discuss whether SCOTUS in effect is a complex adaptive system. Consider such decisions as Plessy v. Ferguson (1896) and more recent civil rights decisions. Consider the components of a complex system; how do they fit or not fit?[1]
2. Apply complexity to understand social service program functioning. This brief exercise begins the process of framing social service phenomena into a complexity perspective. To

Table 2.1 Prompts When Identifying Components of a Complex System

Complexity Component and Prompts	Application
Agent-Based • Who is the intended audience? • Is the unit of analysis individuals, families, or groups? • Are these agents able to make decisions?	
Attraction • Why are clients seeking services?	
Self-Organizing • What keeps clients motivated to continue or complete services? • What is the client's level of functioning when beginning the social service?	
Boundaries • What are the simple rules governing the agents' behaviors? • What heuristics contribute to emergent behavior?	
Feedback • Do program staff members use the client's strengths, needs, abilities, and preferences? • Does the organization's array of services reflect their clients' preferences?	
Emergent Behavior • Are clients with similar characteristics grouping together? • Do client outcomes reflect any pattern? • Do client outcomes reflect their strengths, preferences, and abilities?	

begin, students should identify an experience from their past work history or field experience in order to deconstruct elements from the experience into the components that comprise a CAS. In the worked example of this exercise, I use information obtained from a large two county organization working with persons who have an intellectual disability. The services provided by the organization include housing supports, employment and educational services, and assorted supports to assist these individuals in living independently in their communities. Using Table 2.1, state how the various components of complexity theory apply to a field placement of a social service situations in which you may have been involved. If possible, please state any suggested prompts to help others identify these components.

WORKED EXAMPLE: HOW COMPLEXITY COMPONENTS APPLY TO HOUSING FOR PERSONS WITH DISABILITIES

Agent-Based

- Who is the intended audience? The primary audience is people with disabilities living in the community.
- Is the unit of analysis individuals, families, or groups? The unit of analysis in this model is groups, which agents group with which agents. However, a large amount of the focus is on the individual composition of the groups—whether the groups are made up mostly of people with disabilities or people without disabilities.
- Are these agents able to make decisions? They are able to make very limited decisions, their decisions are largely based on the rules of the program and the movement of other agents but there is some room for decision-making. This includes where they move and which groups they join.

Attraction

- Why are the clients seeking services? Clients and/or their advocates sought participation in the services because of their desire to have housing options in the community.

Self-Organizing

- How did self-organization occur? Clients housing preferences led them to certain decisions. These decisions were based on simple rules related to zoning, transit, and availability of additional support services.

Boundaries

- What are the simple rules governing the agents' behaviors? The simple rules are to form groups, expend, and take in energy; if connected to another agent then mirror that agent's movements.
- What heuristics contribute to the emergent behavior? None.

Feedback

- Do program staff members use the client's strengths, needs, abilities, and preferences? Program staff do not really factor into the model. The agents without disabilities are supposed to be community members; no staff members are factored into the model.
- Does the organization's array of services reflect their clients' preferences? An array of services is not really being offered in the model, just the self-determination to join whatever group the client chooses to join, so in that regard the program provides that one service based on the preferences of the client.

Emergent Behavior

- Are clients with similar characteristics grouping together? They are. The graph in the model is tracking the numbers of clients that group together based on their shared connection with community members or lack of a connection. Those that have a connection group with community members they are connected with, while those without the connection group with other clients that do not have the connection.
- Do client outcomes reflect any pattern? A pattern does emerge that shows that the clients with connections to community members are more likely to group with community members than clients without links to community members.
- Do client outcomes reflect their strengths, preferences, and abilities? The outcomes seem to reflect their preferences; however, whether it reflects their strengths and abilities is unclear.

3

Research and Evaluation Methods for Complexity

An old idiom posits that when earning a PhD, students learn more and more about less and less, until they know everything about nothing. Unfortunately, this may not be far from the truth. Developing the abilities and skills to learn a topic deeply is an essential skill, though, unfortunately, we often become too focused and reductionist. Approaches to complexity oriented research address this trend by using the benefits derived from multiple methods and multidisciplinary collaboration.

The examples provided in this chapter benefitted from the diverse perspectives of people from different levels within ecosystems and from information garnered from other disciplines. This chapter introduces current methods used in investigating social work related issues that are framed as complex systems. Complexity oriented inquiry blends quantitative and qualitative methods. The examples in this chapter reinforce many of the concepts introduced in the first two chapters by applying the materials to social service phenomena. Researching complexity does not take a singular qualitative or quantitative orientation, and involves both inductive and deductive reasoning.

Learning objectives for this chapter include

- the ability to develop research questions applicable to a complex systems framework;
- an understanding of the qualitative and quantitative research methods used to analyze complexity.

It's not the team with the best players; it's the players with the best team who win the Stanley Cup.

—Neale, 1997

Social work's underlying premise of person-in-environment conforms to the general framework of complexity. Inherently as social workers, we understand the influences of multiple systems interacting. Because of this, multiple research areas within our field avail themselves to applying the concepts identified in this book. When reading this chapter, you should realize that each of the research and evaluation methods discussed reflect complexity because each uses client level data, produces change, and benefits from the diverse perspectives of the participants.

TYPES OF SOCIAL WORK QUESTIONS ADDRESSED BY A COMPLEXITY METHOD

To pique your interests in applying complexity, we can start with eco-maps, which most social work students had to develop in either an early methods or human behavior in the social environment course. To demonstrate, this application of a social service phenomenon included where people with intellectual and developmental disabilities lived relative to several variables. These variables—including the involvement of allies of the person with disabilities in planning for their futures, their level of disability, the number of others with a disability living in the same home, and the percentage of earned income to total income—continued to provide a strong basis for applying nonlinear methods.

Egocentric social networks (discussed more thoroughly in chapter 4) suggest one viable approach to investigating the strength of supports that individuals may receive from their families and friends as they cooperatively plan and participate in social service interventions. In egocentric social networks, the network surrounds an individual (in this instance the person with a disability, or the ego), and the influences from those surrounding the individual (alters). From this initial schema, further study can inquire into the evolution of service delivery provided to the person, the person's relationship to the surrounding environment, the robustness and resiliency of the person to threats which may arise (potentially moderated because of the strength of the person's supports), and finally how the influences of location affect the person's interactions with the community. In chapter 7, these variables are modeled to provide a worked example of agent-based modeling (ABM). Before moving to ABM, it is valuable to demonstrate how the study of complexity can be initiated with research and evaluation methods familiar to most graduate students and researchers. This chapter applies several methods to inquire how these well-known strategies can initiate your application of research within a complex systems framework.

INTEGRATION OF QUALITATIVE AND QUANTITATIVE METHODS

The methods below—including participatory action research, narrative, emergent design, social network analysis, cluster analysis, and spatial analysis—demonstrate how complexity has been applied in several social service research and evaluation settings. These methods are not meant to be an exhaustive list, but rather they provide a few examples of how complexity theory was used metaphorically. These methods demonstrate that they are complementary. Readers seeking detailed explanations of the specific methods should refer to the sources provided. Of significant importance is the possibility that complexity theory can blend the respective benefits of qualitative and quantitative research methods. Qualitative research has the characteristics of applying inductive reasoning to social work processes, and using non-numerical data to answer exploratory inquiries. Conversely, quantitative research often relies on a deductive approach and applies numerical data to measure outcomes through hypothesis testing (Rubin & Babbie, 2008).

Participatory Action Research

As social workers, we appreciate and use information from persons served and others who have the closest contact with services. Stringer's (1999) working principles of community-based action research align well with this complex systems approach to evaluation. He states that effective action research involves maximizing the involvement of all relevant individuals; includes all groups affected; includes relevant social, economic, cultural, and political issues; ensures cooperation with other groups; and ensures that all relevant groups benefit from the activities.

Initially, action research evolved from efforts of teachers, school administrators, and students to improve classroom performance (Mertler, 2006). These efforts centered on applying research methods to actual practice environments. In the past decade or two, action research applications have spread throughout social and health services, business, and other arenas. As with many systems improvement approaches that continually use feedback, action research involves iterative cycles of diagnosing (defining the problem or need), planning action, taking action, evaluating action, and evaluating whether the process changes the diagnosis. It is this final link of the evaluating action—determining whether the initial diagnosis has changed—that is frequently overlooked.

Participatory action research involves a series of action steps to ensure the involvement of community members in this bottom-up approach (Homan, 2011). First, community members need to determine the focus of the effort. The second step involves determining what is known and unknown, and from this determination a goal is selected to investigate. Constructing a hypothesis, based on what community members know, serves as the next step. Identifying the available and obtainable resources leads to selecting an approach to implement the action research strategy. The person(s) leading the action research efforts in collaboration with the key constituents then develops the plan to test the effectiveness of the chosen strategy. The researchers and others involved implement the strategy and collect data, which leads to analyzing the results in collaboration with the key constituents to assess what happened. These results are shared with the key constituents to determine what was learned and this knowledge guides further action. Throughout this process, information is provided from those most involved, and several iterations provide feedback for refinement.

This first application of a method sought to improve the use of fixed route public transit systems (including buses and trains) for these persons with disabilities, rather than have them use paratransit services. In this application, local planners provided travel training services, the professional activity that instructs people with disabilities on how to travel independently on fixed route transit. Travel training services are normally provided and funded by school districts, social service organizations, and transportation authorities. While people enroll in travel training programs for a variety of reasons, many are interested in learning how to use a fixed route in lieu of paratransit for some or all of their trips. People with disabilities increase their community independence by using fixed route transit for several reasons, including not having to schedule a ride a day in advance, and having more reliable schedules. This has the additional benefit of reducing resource expenditures of local transportation providers, and contributes to the sustainability of local transport systems. To address this issue, Wolf-Branigin, Wolf-Branigin, culver, and Welch (2012) developed a generalized cost–benefit model based on the feedback of providers and riders of the systems. The results support the emerging field by contributing to the body of knowledge and giving decision makers the feedback needed to make good business decisions. Travel training is a new professional field with an emerging body of knowledge on theory, practice, and research. A cost–benefit model was applied to understand the value of travel training services and the implications for public transportation agencies. We found that providing this service saved the funding bodies resources and improved the ability of persons with disabilities to be increasingly engaged with their communities. (Those seeking additional information on participatory action research should refer to Stinger, 1999, or Coghlan and Brannick, 2005.)

Narrative Approach

Based upon a researcher's experiences, the narrative approach seeks to understand how a social work phenomena functions as a complex system. This method will be the most metaphorical of the approaches discussed in this chapter. Studies conducted under a narrative approach may include autoethnography, where the experiences and the perceptions of the writer deeply explain a phenomenon through a recursive process.

As an example, for the past few years I have been working on an autoethnography within a complex systems framework that applies conflict, cooperation, and then creativity on two emerging issues from the deinstitutionalization period of the 1970s: the shift towards community inclusion and improving quality of life for persons with developmental disabilities. I lived with a young adult who had an intellectual and developmental disability for 18 months in what was called in that time period a normalization apartment. The project's goal was to illustrate changes that occurred by including my roommate in my daily life. While the initiative's activities facilitated community participation and normalization of my roommate—a young adult with multiple disabilities—it began to empower him to live in increasingly less restrictive environments. (Those seeking additional information on narrative analysis should refer to Czarniawaska, 2004.)

Emergent Design Process/Developmental Evaluation

Understanding the preferences and needs of persons using services results in efficiencies and increases their buy-in to the services. In this study, the evaluators were asked by a state Medicaid office to design a system of improved access for persons with severe physical disabilities as the current system was shifting to a managed care approach. Using an emergent design process, several focus groups were conducted with individuals who access the Medicaid services statewide (Wolf-Branigin & LeRoy, 2004). Results from the focus groups indicated two main concerns. First, was the desire to initiate one-on-one advocacy to improve local service coordination, and the second was an interest in conducting person-centered planning at the time of enrollment into one of the Medicaid managed care plans in order to facilitate appropriate and prompt access.

Based on these expressed desires, and with input from the evaluators, the state Medicaid managed care system agreed to test whether using physiatrists (physicians specializing in physical disabilities) rather than general practitioners produced a better response to the individuals' needs. The physiatrists better understood the various drug interactions and their effects on persons with severe disabilities and, as a result. actual Medicaid expenditures were reduced because of fewer hospitalizations for secondary conditions (e.g., medication interactions and bedsores), even though the physiatrists had a greater initial cost. (For more information on developmental evaluation, please refer to Patton, 2011.)

Building Robust Social Networks

Networks play an essential role in maintaining and monitoring systems. To demonstrate this, we used a developmental evaluation approach to measure the increased resilience of immigrant teenagers. In this study, resilience was reframed as the concept of system robustness. This included focusing on how "small world" and scale free networks function better than random networks. This included the concept of complex networks (Barabasi, 2002; Watts & Strogatz, 1998) with a focus on power laws and the growth and preferential attachment that need to occur in developing complex networks. The conceptual aspect of "small world networks" focused on the desire to create additional linkages or interconnections with individuals and institutions with whom the adolescent could contact. The creation of additional linkages improves an individual's robustness by increasing access to educational, training, and employment opportunities.

Similar to the Settlement House Movement of the late 1800s in the United States and England, the program design linked recent immigrants with well-established individuals and institutions in order to alleviate social disintegration (Axinn & Stern, 2008). These programs were based in the voluntary not-for-profit sector, and the services were oriented toward social change by envisioning the family as the core social structure, one to be stabilized and strengthened through linking with families of different social status (Husock, 1992). It is suggested that the Settlement House approach serves as a model to be revisited (Lundblad, 1995). This design again attests to the desire for creating robust social systems emerging from the basic unit (the family) to create an emergent behavior of a more civil and inclusive society.[1]

The developmental evaluation produced more than the findings about progress. More important, materials useful for program development emerged that indicated the programs required timely engagement and rapid feedback. Developmental evaluation can become an engine for the project with program development and evaluation becoming mutually reinforcing. The developmental evaluation assumed a systems change approach combined with collaboration (Patton, 2011). The systems change aspect included the perspectives, boundaries, and interrelationships wherein social innovators (organizational staff) envision a system they find unacceptable, and then modify the system (acculturation of immigrant youth). The collaborative aspect focuses on networking, cooperation, and collaborating.

Cluster Analysis

K-means cluster analysis has application to complexity theory because of its ability to identify how groups form in a two-dimensional physical space.

A study using a two-step cluster analysis explored whether natural groupings or clusters of homes for persons with developmental disabilities occurred based on the number of individuals residing in the homes (Wolf-Branigin, 2006). A log-likelihood distance measure (the physical distances between the homes) was used to create probability distributions of the variables, and clustering criteria assessed whether homes were spatially dependent based on the number of people residing within each location. Initially four clusters were created: one-person homes (n = 43), two- to four-person (n = 64) homes, five-person homes (n = 62), and six- to eight-person homes (n = 125). Distance measures were based on a log-likelihood approach with the assumption in independence between variables.

Results indicated that persons with an intellectual disability who were living independently resided in the more densely populated portions of the region. Their choice of housing options tended to occur closer to transit lines so that they could more freely travel to their employment, educational, and other systems. The emergent pattern revealed that larger homes had greater mean distances from their respective group centroid (the mean location within a cluster). These greater distances potentially indicate more isolation from the community at large. This was especially true for the three- and four-person homes. This dispersion may have been attributed to larger homes having their own transportation (vans) and, therefore, they could be located farther from the public transportation often found in more densely populated areas. Group centroids likewise indicated that all people who were living independently resided in the more densely populated areas. (For additional information on cluster analysis, please refer to Tabachnick and Fidell, 2001.)

Spatial Analysis

The Macomb-Oakland Regional Center in suburban Detroit has been facilitating the movement of persons with developmental disabilities into the community for more than three decades. The community inclusion movement for people with developmental disabilities is predicated on the assumption that all individuals have the right to be fully participating citizens of their communities. This shift to increasing citizenship was encouraged and exemplified by modifications in employment, housing, and educational policies, as well as other services affecting people with developmental disabilities.

To measure the randomness of their home locations, a geographic-based spatial analytic approach was used. The involvement of allies in planning for the future, the number of people with disabilities residing in each home, the proportion of earned income, level of disability, and level of mobility were all used as explanatory variables. Monte Carlo procedures using Moran's I (a measure of spatial autocorrelation) did not reveal significant clustering of residences. Regression procedures, however, did reveal that earned income was the independent variable that most explained the degree to which people were physically included. People living in smaller homes were more randomly dispersed. As self-determination and consumer-focused planning techniques became widespread, people with disabilities explored and participated in their community; sought new experiences; and learned how to live, work, recreate, and go to school with peers who did not have disabilities.

Quantifying locations allows spatial features to be geographically referenced and mapped. This quantification of attributes facilitates the identification and analysis of spatial relationship distributions (Chou, 1997). Whereas regression analysis models typically have been built to explain the distribution of phenomenon (dependent variable), location and attribute data can be studied to understand spatial distributions and interrelationships of people with disabilities (Chou, 1997). Spatial methods focusing on the relationships between coordinates are referred to as point pattern analysis, which is often the first step in identifying whether some factor or variable is causing first-order patterning or clustering (Cressie, 1993).

This emerging community inclusion context for persons with disabilities reflects self-determination, individualized budgets, and consumer-focused planning techniques (Nerney, Crowley, & Kappel, 1995). As people with disabilities are encouraged to explore and connect with their community, seek new experiences, learn how to live, work, enjoy recreation activities, and attend schools that are not segregated by whether a student has a disability or not, these individuals are afforded opportunities to become fully participating citizens. The interest in such decentralized planning approaches grew from a concern that professionals in government-funded organizations were often unable to provide the personal commitment people need as they become more involved in their community. These efforts help secure community jobs and housing, and more people with disabilities are in competitive employment and independent housing (Braddock, 2002), becoming fully included in their communities. (For a detailed resource on spatial analysis, refer to Bailey and Gatrell,1995.)

SUMMARY

This chapter presented an overview of six studies that applied the complexity paradigm in their social program evaluations. The studies ranged from a highly qualitative narrative approach, to a computationally intensive spatial analysis method. The salient point is that complexity provides a flexible framework for conducting inquiry. Chapter 4 shifts the focus to specific statistical and mathematical approaches to measuring complexity. By focusing on individual level information and decisions gained from game theory, we will begin to better understand how decisions made by individuals lead to an emergent behavior.

EXERCISES

1. Develop a research question from your past or current agenda that uses complexity theory as the undergirding approach. What current research methods would you use? Identify who you would collaborate with outside of social work?[2]
2. When discussing how interconnectedness assists in building a robust system, explain how, given that the Social Security system provides universal coverage, this makes it more robust?
3. Go to the Educause Review Online website (http:// www.educause.edu/EDUCAUSE+Review/ EDUCAUSEReviewMagazineVolume44/ AwebGameforPredictingSomeFutur/171494) and create a model with a cooperative aspect. You can go with the flow, or bid with everyone, or you can bid against or sell short on the market. If you bid (cooperate) with everyone else, you boost the values of your options and you get rich; if you sell short or bid on options

that the majority did not bid on, it negatively affects the value of your highest option, but it may provide a larger payoff for you at the expense of everyone else. This could be an interactive project to explore the meaning of the prisoner's dilemma and facilitate discussion on why someone would choose to cooperate or not.

4

Shifting from a Metaphorical to a Mathematical Approach

Before moving on to a research method developed to understand complex systems (agent-based modeling), a few mathematical and statistical concepts that support investigating complex phenomena within social work need reinforcing. This chapter reviews several of these concepts so that readers may apply them more readily when investigating complexity. Reviewing and building upon these mathematical concepts aids in understanding complex networks and the interconnected environments in which social workers conduct their practices and research.

After completing chapter 4, readers will have

- a preliminary understanding of the mathematical concepts behind complexity theory;
- an understanding the role of game theory—through cooperative and competitive games—in the development of complexity;
- the ability to link these mathematical concepts to social service applications.[1]

In Pixar's animated feature film, *Ratatouille* (Lewis & Bird, 2007), food critic Alton Ego asks for "perspective" from an emerging chef. As a result of this request, Alton is "brought back home," because of a simple dish the chef created that reminds him of his childhood. In much the same manner, I intend to bring social work students—who have long feared mathematical concepts—back home, so they can gain perspective and apply lessons they learned during adolescence.

For a quarter century, the field of social program evaluation sought a unifying approach that could integrate various methodologies for investigating complex social service systems (Wooldridge, 1981). Integrating such diverse research and evaluative methodologies—that used both qualitative and quantitative approaches—into a coherent evaluative strategy required that such an approach be sensitive to time and location. Chapter 4 discusses these issues toward developing an overall framework for the use of complexity in social service inquiry. Turner (2001) explains social work theory as the set of testable explanations based on professional activities that we perform for and with the stakeholders to whom we are accountable. This demands that we identify ways to gather homogenous data that allows us to abstract indicators of successful outcomes and tie these into differential theory outcomes.

This chapter emerged as our department of social work began planning a doctoral curriculum. I was assigned the task of preparing the research methods and statistics classes. As you may understand, I had a strong interest in designing an advanced statistics class in nonlinear methods. In preparing coursework, my desire to keep the material centered on the following four aspects was paramount:

- Knowing your client or organization's current functioning level
- Identifying what attracts a client or organization to be involved
- Ascertaining how other clients and organizations then self-organize
- Seeing how this leads to an emergent collective behavior

MATHEMATICAL CONCEPTS RELATED TO COMPLEXITY

Data analysis methods for complexity typically reflect an exploratory approach rather than a traditional hypothesis testing or confirmatory approach. A complexity framework shifts the typical social work research question of comparing groups or seeking linear relationships vis-à-vis ANOVA or regression models, respectively, to one that identifies and quantifies trends (e.g., seasonal variation), applies spatial analysis (clustering on occurrences), or identifies nested phenomena using hierarchical linear modeling (HLM). HLM extends regression frameworks beyond predicting past group behavior to more clearly accounting for variation at different levels or contexts of social groups. Rather than seeking linear relationships or significant group differences, complexity uses statistical methods by predicting group membership (e.g., discriminate functions), identifying underlying structure (e.g., exploratory factor analysis), or discerning a time course of events (Tabachnick & Fidell, 2001). Several mathematical influences upon which the study of complex systems is based are now introduced and reviewed.

Boolean Logic

This branch of mathematics, named for Charles Boole, who was instrumental in developing the field of formal logic in the mid 1800s, relates closely to relational algebra and set theory. Rather than having the basic algebraic operations of addition, subtraction, multiplication, and division; Boolean logic uses AND, OR, NOT. This may be most familiar to you when performing a literature search. Similar to algebra, Boolean logic is the branch of mathematics that uses binary formulas using the constants "0" and "1" rather than numbers. These binary digits (bits) continue in importance today as we live in a binary or digital environment. One simple example is hypothesis testing. This branch of mathematics provides the means to code decision rules into computational models.

Decision Theory

This branch of mathematics and statistics investigates the values, uncertainties, and other issues related to how individuals, groups, or organizations make a decision, the reasons behind the decision, and the best or optimal decision that results. Decision theory closely relates to game theory. A simple example that we are all familiar with is getting Type I and Type II errors when determining whether to accept or reject a null hypothesis. Of all the mathematical concepts stated here, decision science most aligns with statistics, because it seeks to identify the best decision that is likely to occur.

Decision theory closely relates to game theory because the interactions of agents, who probably have conflicting interests, make decisions that affect other agents. Decision theory consists of two branches, normative and descriptive. The normative branch identifies the best decision to make based on having complete information and with the agent being fully rational. Descriptive, also known as positive decision theory, seeks to describe what actual agents do given that they either act irrationally or lack complete information (Peterson, 2009).

Graph Theory

Based on the work in the seventeenth century mathematician Leonhard Euler, who investigated movement across bridges and identifying the shortest path, this branch of mathematics studies graphs as mathematical structures (Newman, 2010). These graphs provide the basis for the study of networks because they consist of vertices (nodes) and links (edges) between nodes. Graph theory provides the vehicle for drawing and formalizing these important connections because social work uses a person-in-environment (PIE) perspective. Graph theory provides the theoretical basis for network science and provides an essential tool for identifying the interconnections prevalent in complex systems.

SOCIAL NETWORK ANALYSIS

The social network analysis (SNA) perspective provides a strong methodological approach that is consistent with complexity. Not to be confused with popular electronic social networking sites such as Facebook or Twitter (although these too are social networks), SNA shifts from a simple orientation of *who knows who*, to an orientation that more deeply seeks to understand *who knows who knows whom*. In SNA, effects of networking can be easily realized to matters in which there are three degrees of influence.

This social science research methodology parallels complexity well, as the next several paragraphs will attest. Briefly, this relational approach studies the connections within systems. It assumes that social units are interdependent and have multiple levels of relational properties. These social networks in addition to providing positive linkages also contain contagions.

Several rules of life are found in social networks (Christakis & Fowler, 2009). Quite simply these may be summarized as (1) we shape our networks, (2) our networks shape us, (3) our friends affect us, (4) our friends' friends affect us, and (5) the network has a life of its own—it displays emergent properties. As a quick reading of this indicates, these rules are consistent with the simple notions found in complex systems because of the interdependencies, interconnectedness, the use of feedback, and the creation of an emergent behavior.

Social network analysis likewise operates under several assumptions. First, there are *actors* (clients, groups) who have interdependent actions. These actors are represented as *nodes (vertices)*. Second, there are *ties* between actors that serve as channels for resource flows. These ties, edges, or links are represented as *lines*. These network ties have the dual effect of both enabling and constraining action in much the same way that simple rules affect complex systems. The *structure* emerging from the network is viewed as an enduring relational pattern.

The study of social networks involves the structural concepts defined using *graph theory* and *matrix operations*. Graph theory provides a formal (mathematical) representation of networks. These graphs may be directional (where information flows in one direction) and/or nondirectional (when information flows in both directions). The degree of a node (D [n1]) refers to the number of lines attached to a node. These ties can be either undirected or directed. In a directed graph, the ties have two types of degrees, in-degree and out-degree (Newman, 2010).

Representing networks in the simplest terms includes two types of components, *nodes* and *links*. Nodes are individuals or groups being studied, whereas the links (lines, ties, edges) represent the connections. The links themselves may be directional or not.

Transitivity and *connectivity* become another important concept in social network analysis. This concept briefly states that if A=B, and B=C, then A=C, and implies that the necessary ties emerge from networks. Connectivity, which builds upon the concept of transitivity, refers to the indirect connections between nodes traced along paths, where the graph (geodesic) distance between the nodes equals the number of ties between the nodes, for one person is connected to another.

Connectedness represents interconnections and interactions that provide experiences to persons in the network that are not available to the individuals themselves. The connectivity of a graph refers to whether the graph remains connected when nodes and/or lines are deleted. This introduces two additional terms related to nodes and links: *cutpoint* and *bridge*. A node is a cutpoint when it reduces the number of components in subgraph. A line is a bridge when its removal results in fewer components. *Node-connectivity* and *line-connectivity* are terms with similar outcomes. Node-connectivity refers to the minimum number (k) of nodes that must be removed to disconnect the graph. Conversely, line-connectivity is the minimum number (l) of lines that must be removed to disconnect the graph.

Matrices and *matrix operations* provide mathematical grounding for the application of multivariate statistical methods. Although rarely addressed in social work statistics and research methods courses, obtaining a rudimentary understanding deepens our understanding of mathematical statistics. Basic matrix operations include transposing and multiplying matrices. Although embedded in the data analysis software packages used in social network analysis, matrix operations are essential in calculating centrality and centralization. Similarly, measures have been developed to account for the prestige of individual nodes (agents). The primary measure is referred to as centrality and can be measured in three ways, degree, closeness, or betweenness.

Two broad categories or types of networks are analyzed: whole network and egocentric networks. Whole networks, also referred to as complete or saturated, inquire into the connections of all members within a given population. Whole networks are used to look at the possible ties between all members. The focus of analysis is on sub-graphs called either dyads or triads. Dyads look at the types of patterns present in pairs of people or agents, whereas triads look into the patterns in the relationships between three individuals or agents.

Ego-centered social network analysis focuses on an individual agent (ego), and inquires into the local ties around ego. This branch of social network analysis will be most useful when the units of analysis are individuals or families.

Social network analysis provides potential applications for social work researchers and evaluation. Analyzing whole system networks concerns the flow of resources in a larger network. For example, a county or regional authority may be curious how the human service organizations that they contract interact. In this case, the governmental unit may monitor how clients served through their contracted network of services are referred and what kind of continuum of care they receive a continuum from the different organization contracted to provide services. The unit may also check to assure that the subcontracted organizations have formal referral agreements with one another to increase the likelihood of an efficient and effective referral process for exchange on client information. Subgraphs would be used in this instance to study the types or patterns of relationships within a whole system.

Social networks display complexity where agents are linked by a common action or interest. These agents have some form of shared communication, membership or other form of exchange (Manheim, Rich, Willnat, & Brians, 2006). SNA helps to assess information sharing and knowledge creation that results from group interactions. The preceding was a very brief introduction to the growing field of social network analysis. Those seeking additional information of the application of SNA to practice should review Christakis and Fowler (2009) and Knoke and Yang (2008), while those who want to go more in-depth concerning methodology are referred to Newman (2010) and to Wasserman and Faust (1994).

Spatial Autocorrelation

Spatial analysis encompasses a variety of tools for identifying the role of space or location on explicitly specified spatial variables in the explanation or prediction of phenomenon (Kettner, Moroney, & Martin, 2013) and provides an interactive framework to understand many geographic processes and dependencies (clustering). These dependencies often are represented as clusters. Assessing *spatial autocorrelation*, the extent to which the occurrence of an event in one area (for example, housing) is influenced by the distribution of similar features in a neighboring area, is one method for understanding these dependencies. A branch of spatial analysis, spatial autocorrelation has particular application to complexity and its use in social work research.

In the following application of spatial autocorrelation, the primary objective was to determine, whether housing patterns for persons with a disability were clustered or random. Because the desired outcome was for these persons to be included in their communities, we were expecting to have a lack of clustering. Although similar applications of spatial autocorrelation have been applied to a variety of situations, including transportation (Koenig, 1980), genetic structure (Epperson & Li, 1996), and health care (Martin & Williams, 1992), such methods had not been used to measure community inclusion. Assuming the organization's goal of community inclusion, the objective was to find an absence of clustering or autocorrelation.

A common statistic measuring spatial autocorrelation is Moran's I (Cressie, 1993), which is essentially a Pearson product-moment correlation coefficient requiring interval-level observations, and modified to account for a spatial weight matrix (Gettis, 1991). Values may range from −1 to 1. A high value (approaching 1.0) indicates a clustered pattern, whereas a low value (approaching −1) indicates a scattered pattern. A value near zero indicates randomness. As individuals become more included in their communities, the objective is for patterns to approximate zero.

Computational Theory

Although the computational nature of complex adaptive systems may strike fear in many, it provides a valuable bottom–up framework that accounts for individual client (agent) behavior, resulting in larger patterns, rather than the top–down approach of the testing of models. It potentially provides a more sensitive method for investigating individuals and their responses to social interventions. Using Miller and Page's (2007)—part approach to explain their method, this section introduces readers to essential concepts of computation. While several of these concepts may initially be unfamiliar to social work researchers (e.g., cellular automata, self-organized criticality, and emergence theory), these concepts nonetheless are essential to grasping and applying complexity components. When garnering an understanding of complexity, several scholarly publications stress the importance of understanding the evolution of computational theory from mathematics (Gleick, 2011; Johnson, 2007; Mitchell, 2009).

Claude Shannon's work in communication theory largely influenced the field of computational theory (Shannon, & Weaver, 1949). This pioneering work can be seen in how we search digitalized databases through the application of the Boolean operations AND, OR,

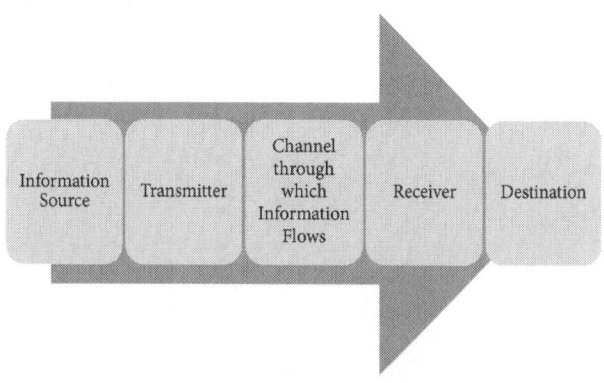

Figure 4.1 Diagram of Communication Theory.

NOT when seeking evidence on a selected topic (Cournoyer, 2004). According to Shannon, a communication system must contain five elements, an information source, the transmitter, the channel, the receiver, and the destination (see Figure 4.1). The information source includes the person generating the message or information. This may consist of a series of characters, mathematical symbols. The transmitter is what encodes the message by producing a signal that can later be decoded. The channel simply refers to the medium over which the message is transmitted. The receiver reverses what the transmitter did by decoding the signal. Finally, the destination is the person at the end receiving the message or signal.

All of the above leads us to consider what computation is and what the limits are to it? The discussion really begins with the work of the mathematicians Hilbert, Gödel, and Turing from the early to mid twentieth century. In the beginning of the twentieth century, German mathematician David Hilbert posed a series of three questions:

1. Is mathematics complete (can any mathematical statement be proven or not given a set of axioms)?
2. Is mathematics consistent (can only true statements be proven)?
3. Can every statement in mathematics be decided (is there a certain procedure that can be applied to a mathematical statement that will tell us whether it is true or not)?

Hilbert believed the answer to all three questions was yes, and concluded that no problem could go unresolved. By 1930, however, the mathematician and logician Kurt Godel surprised the mathematics field by proving the incompleteness theorem, which in effect stated that if the answer to Hilbert's second question was yes (is mathematics consistent?), then the answer to the first question must be no (is mathematics complete?). In summary, this states that a mathematical system can be consistent or complete, but it can never accomplish both simultaneously. The importance of this lies in disproving mathematically that mathematics was something perfect. Although Hilbert had initially attempted to tidy up some loose ends, his work introduced a new level of noise or complexity into mathematics.

This development leads to the British mathematician Alan Turing, widely regarded as the father of modern computing who created a machine that led to cellular automata. From the preceding discussion, the concept of cellular automata emerged. This centers on how the change in one organism affects the surrounding ones. In computational theory, this involves an "if—then" command. As noted above, Hilbert's third question includes the notion of a definite procedure.

Turing developed the conceptual blueprint for the electronic programmable computer. This work, conducted by Turing during World War II, was instrumental in breaking the German *Enigma* machine codes. His accomplishments have been credited with providing great assistance in winning World War II by cracking the Enigma code. Without cracking this code, the German U-boats could not be stopped, and without stopping them, the United Kingdom could not be supplied, and the Normandy Day invasion could not have been successful.

Much of this discussion on the development of information and computational theory leads to two important concepts essential to applying complex systems to social work. The first, *self-organized criticality,* refers to a property in dynamical systems that have a critical point (tipping point) as an attractor. Such behavior displays the time and space characteristic of the point at which the system changes, but without controlling the limits at precise values. The second concept, *emergence theory*, arose from the self-organizing behavior. This includes the structures and functions that arise from the interactions of agents.

In computational theory, it is essential to have flexibility rather than precision, so that a wider range of behaviors can be included and be process oriented while not being oversimplified or reductionist. Computational concepts are relatively new to most social workers. Computation theory, in its simplest form, relays information with as few characters or symbols as possible. As an example that many of us have encountered, when and if we've traveled to Manhattan and sought half-price tickets in the theater district, the common approach is to go to the "TKTS" windows located at Times Square. The shortened term "TKTS" is easily recognizable as tickets.

LINKING CONCEPTS TO RESEARCH APPROACHES

A framework for applying computational complexity emerges as we begin understanding the mathematical and conceptual influences upon which the study of complexity is based. General systems theory and ecosystems theory equips social workers with an undergirding framework for understanding vital PIE interactions, but this framework poses difficulties as we attempt to quantify phenomenon over time and location. This section briefly reviews the concepts of complex systems that are used when researching or evaluating social work phenomena. We then apply a variety of statistical methods to use when measuring the various components of complexity and emergence. While these methods assist in measuring complexity, it is in chapter 6 (agent-based modeling) where we will apply the concepts of emergence and self-organizing behaviors more accurately to build predictive models based on the rules of system behavior or the bottom–up decisions of individual agents.

Complexity has become an accepted theoretical paradigm within the natural sciences where advanced agent-based modeling programs predict emergent behaviors (Epstein, 1999; Grimm et al., 2005; Gorman, Mezik, Mezik, & Gruenewald, 2006). Its assumptions and applications, however, pose significant challenges to social service research and evaluation. To apply a strong quantitative complexity framework, we need to shift from a pure hypothesis-testing approach to pattern-recognition exploratory studies that can identify nonlinearity.

Contemporary social work research and evaluation encourages the use of mixed-methods by applying both qualitative and quantitative approaches when examining the effects of social programs (Creswell, 2003); they use these methods separately and, therefore, they lack integration between the qualitative and quantitative data. The proposed framework for applying complexity to human service organizations provides a possible solution to this dilemma by integrating a mixed-model approach, using both qualitative-based process information and quantitative-based outcome measures that can encourage program sustainability (Westley, Zimmerman, & Patton, 2006).

Social work researchers use increasingly advanced statistical techniques, but these methods often lack the sensitivity to identify emergent self-organizing behaviors. This remains especially true in determining the needs of at-risk populations. Broader impacts from the proposed activities are needed to expand on the current human service research approaches that focus solely on experimental and quasi-experimental methods. As social work researchers and educators apply complex systems approaches, rigorous methods provide new insights into human service phenomenon.

Methods need to reflect that data analysis within complexity assumes an exploratory or pattern-recognition approach rather than a traditional hypothesis-testing or confirmatory approach. Complexity shifts social workers' research questions from ones of comparing groups or seeking linear relationships vis-à-vis ANOVA and regression models respectively, to ones that look at trends (e.g., seasonal variation), spatial relationships (clustering on occurrences), and nested phenomena in hierarchical linear models (HLM), which extends regression frameworks beyond predicting past group behavior to more clearly accounting for variations at different levels in social groups.

Rather than seeking linear relationships or significant group differences, complexity applies statistical methods of predicting group membership (e.g., discriminate functions), identifying underlying structure (e.g., exploratory factor analysis), or discerning a time course of events (Tabachnick & Fidell, 2001). This framework provides for the development of spatial methods to predict and quantify social work phenomena within often apparently chaotic environments. Figure 4.2 applies several of these concepts to a social service organization providing support services to persons with intellectual and developmental disabilities.

Measuring Sensitivity to Initial Conditions

Multiple software options are available. In addition to using MS Excel or SPSS for basic descriptive and inferential statistics, appropriate and

Complexity Component	Relevance	Suggested Statistical Method
Sensitivity to initial conditions	Discerning background of the agents/clients	Simple descriptive statistics (e.g., Excel, SPSS)
Attraction	Identifying the factors that attract and maintain client involvement	Autocorrelation
Heterogeneity	Identifying choices available and made	Bayesian decision trees
Dynamic use of feedback	Delineating how information flows and decisions made	Network analysis Survival analysis
Adapting/Self-organizing	Identifying patterns of agents	Cluster analysis Structural equation modeling
Emergent behavior/non-linearity	Identifying outcomes of social work phenomena	Spatial analysis Latent growth modeling Agent-based modeling

Figure 4.2 Inferential Statistical Approaches to Measuring Components of Complexity.

rigorous analysis benefit from additional software packages for assessing autocorrelation and emergent behavior. On a qualitative level, the importance of images warrants developing concept maps, eco-maps, or other displays that assist in visualization. *Microsoft Visio* software provides a simple drag and drop approach for creating graphical and visual representations.

Attraction

In addition to descriptive and inferential statistics, data analysis in an emergence framework may focus on either simple *autocorrelation* or *spatial autocorrelation*. Autocorrelation determines how surrounding observations affect the unit under study, while spatial autocorrelation more specifically applies to two- or three-dimensional space within a spatial econometric approach. The choice of a spatial econometric approach occurs because of the technique's expansion of temporal autocorrelation methods. In this agent-based approach, location information at each time interval is plotted into a two-dimensional space for conducting the autocorrelation analysis (Anselin, Florax, & Rey, 2004).

Heterogeneity

Bayesian decision trees provide one means of identifying and assigning the probabilities of differing paths that agents choose. Three concepts are useful to understanding Bayesian methods: (1) *prior probability* refers to the assumption that the model is true prior to data collection, (2) *posterior probability* refers to the probability that a model is correct after data collection, and (3) *likelihood* describes the conditional probability of the data, assuming the model has been developed (Lee, 2004). Compared to classical inferential statistical methods, Bayesian probabilistic inference enables decision making by evaluating the probable success of a model (or set of models), given the available observed data, and develops conclusions using known sample data. For example, individuals seeking substance abuse treatment with multiple issues will follow differing treatment pathways based on issues such as a co-occurring mental illness, involvement in legal systems or family dysfunction being present.

Dynamic Use of Feedback

Two statistical methods appear useful, *survival analysis* and *network analysis*. Survival analysis provides a useful technique for identifying why some agents self-organize and others do not. Network analysis, also known as social network analysis, seeks to identify the relationships between agents (Wasserman & Faust, 1994). This approach provides a useful method in understanding the flows of information—in this instance the feedback in maintaining a system between interconnected agents. Additionally, because of its use of feedback loops in analyzing system performance, researchers may consider the use of systems dynamics modeling to better understand the role of feedback in systems.

Adapting/Self-Organizing

Two advanced statistical methods apply in measuring adaptation/self-organization: *k-means cluster analysis* and *structural equation modeling*

(SEM). First, k-means cluster analysis explores whether natural groupings or clusters appear. It uses a log-likelihood distance measure to create probability distributions of the variables. The clustering criterion assesses whether the agents are spatially dependent on others within each location (Bailey & Gatrell, 1995). The second approach, SEM, produces latent variables based on several observable variables in order to represent an abstract concept. While SEM typically serves a confirmatory approach to modeling, it can also be exploratory (Bollen, 1989). This approach's strength lies in analyzing the covariance of multiple variables, rather than individual observations. The recent advent of symbolic data analysis, which includes principal components, suggests a potential research analysis method for highly complicated and extremely large data sets.

Emergent Behavior

Emergence represents the self-organizing behavior of human service consumers. Measuring emergence, as represented by various temporal and spatial autocorrelation indices, plays a vital role (Morowitz, 2002). Within complexity, spatial data serve as an extension of time series data in order to identify emergence. Single subject/system research designs represent one approach in which social work researchers use time series designs (Bloom, Fischer, & Orme, 2006). This approach uses repeated measures of a client or client system over time (often before, during, and after an intervention to determine how an intervention changed the performance in a person or group. Applying the emergence concept provides an approach for organizational level inquiry because of the physical attributes and patterns resulting from human service interventions (Hudson, 2000).

The first approach, spatial analysis, includes several methods and related software packages. Within spatial analysis, we typically seek pattern recognition or identify clustering by using spatial autocorrelation. Spatial autocorrelation is similar to linear correlation, but it identifies clusters of observations rather than a line, and it quantifies the influence of surrounding observations on our unit of analysis, the agent or client. One software package in particular, *TerraSeer*, visualizes patterns and quantifies significant clustering in data. The *SpaceStat* features within *TerraSeer* allow for the creation of spatial econometric modeling and the creation of local patterns of spatial associations and simulations. These packages allow for geographic information systems to be included.

Latent growth modeling (Meredith & Tisak, 1990), another form of SEM, estimates individual or agent-based longitudinal growth trajectories. This modeling method uses repeated measures of the dependent variable as a function of a causal and complex process. Latent growth modeling has applications when investigating both system growth and change.

The concepts of networks and complexity are interconnected. While this chapter introduced network analysis within a complexity framework, it only touched upon this field of study. As social service professionals, we are encouraged to seek more tools in order to increase our perspectives and our capacity to become better problem solvers. These tools include social network analysis, Boolean functions, and game theory. Many underlying concepts of complexity science—conflict and cooperation, the wisdom of groups, and robustness and resilience—have long been assumptions to good social work practice. While mention is made to issues such as decision-making theory (e.g., van de Luitgaarden, 2009), scant attention has been paid to computational issues.

The ability of CAS and ABM to generalize across a wide range of applications profoundly improves our capacity to evaluate and understand difficult social issues. CAS moves beyond the simple holistic approach of the whole being worth more than the sum of its parts, because the bottom–up (grassroots) modeling focuses on the lower-level entities (agent or client) that comprise the system. This is unlike a traditional or classical research approach that uses a top–down modeling approach, where we attempt to impose models on clients. (Those seeking a more exhaustive discussion of computation are referred to Mitchell, 2009, chapter 4.)

SUMMARY

This chapter reviewed some basic mathematical and theoretical underpinnings of complexity theory.[2] Much of this material may be familiar from your earlier academic career. A vital aspect to remember is that complexity builds from a multi- and inter-disciplinary approach. In chapter 5, several concepts related to complexity are applied to five recent social service evaluations. This will suggest appropriate settings for conducting research and evaluation, using the statistical methods reviewed in this chapter, within a complex systems paradigm. These five examples are but a few of the methods in which complexity theory and mathematical concepts relate to an evaluative framework.[3] Add them to your toolbox.

EXERCISES

1. Most of you at some time during your social work education had to develop an eco-map. As an initial exercise, explain how you envision that eco-maps and egocentric social networks are related.
2. Game theory provides a method and procedures for understanding how individual agents compete with each other or maximize their quest for scarce resources. Using the website for GAMBIT at the California Institute for Technology (http://www.gambit-project.org/doc/index.html), develop a model that represents the competing forces within a social service organization seeking to garner scarce resources.

5

Social Work Applications of Complexity

Complexity can serve as a means to undergird a variety of social work inquiry. This chapter presents a broad range of environments and types of analyses conducted using complexity theory as the foundational framework. Most of these methods are familiar to readers, and they suggest ways of conducting complexity-based inquiry on current skills.

Because this chapter primarily serves to describe applications of complexity in social work inquiry, the essential learning objectives are

- a review of how social work program evaluations can be framed as complex systems;
- an understanding of the broad scope of potential social work research and program evaluation applications;
- an understanding of related complexity theory concepts to program evaluations.

Amongst democratic nations new families are constantly springing up, others are constantly falling away, and all that remain change their condition...
—de Tocqueville, 1840

DIRECT SERVICE APPLICATIONS

Using five recent studies, this chapter demonstrates how several of the complexity theory related concepts have been applied in recent social work research.[1] To add a consistent framework to the discussion, all of the examples presented concentrate on services developed in collaboration with, and provided to, persons with disabilities. The examples further supply evidence for how the conceptual, mathematical, and statistical foundations from the previous chapter apply.

The complexity related concepts addressed in this chapter involve several of the concepts introduced in chapter 1. These include operating on the edge of chaos, conflict–cooperation, diverse perspectives, diverse heuristics for problem solving, robustness and resilience, self-similarity, and scalability. While this is not an exhaustive list, its intent merely suggests how social work researchers may begin conceptualizing a complex systems approach to their practice inquiry. The materials presented provide examples for applying the statistical methods from the previous chapter to social work.

EXAMPLE 1: HISTORICAL/POLICY ANALYSIS—EMERGENCE OF DISABILITY POLICY

My wife, Karen, and I moved to Washington, DC, about a decade ago because she received a Joseph P. Kennedy Jr. Foundation mid-career fellowship to work on Capital Hill. During the intervening year, we had the opportunity to meet a broad range of people integral to the disability movement of the past several years. This brief historical analysis began with receiving a videodisc (Guggenheim, 1999) from Mrs. Eunice Kennedy Shriver and it sparked my interest to delve a bit deeper into the issue. This study began because a few weeks after receiving the disc, I found several speeches that President Kennedy had presented concerning persons with intellectual disabilities. It struck me that during the past half century, our presidents and presidential candidates had stated little about their personal experiences concerning family members with a disability.

Members of Congress from both sides of the aisle at that time had demonstrated their solid and consistent advocacy for policies and programs for the disabled (e.g., Senators Tom Harkin, James Jeffords, Charles Grassley, and Ted Kennedy); however, those seeking the highest office had stated little in recent years. This study began by deconstructing three JFK speeches (Kennedy, 1962, 1963, 1963b) and an interview conducted with Eunice Kennedy Shriver. Several initial themes emerged, including

- we as a wealthy nation can do better;
- this is an international challenge;
- the desire to improve the interconnected role of science, society, and environment.

Despite the current sound bites and politicians' responses toward social services (especially regarding services for persons with disabilities), these replies tell us little about their passion for the subject. We may search their responses to assure they use person-first language, but their words may still appear contrived. Rhetoric has a place in narrative analysis and can inform the electorate (Graham, 1993; Tierney, 2000); what are the true perspectives of the current and emerging political leaders towards disability? JFK used a variety of individuals with expert knowledge and diverse perspectives and heuristics to address the needs of persons with intellectual and developmental disabilities. While not realizing the current exploratory approach of complexity (Page, 2007), he set standards and expectations of what disability advocates should strive toward in the larger context of inclusion.

President Kennedy outlined this as an international challenge, with a goal for the United States to become the international leader in the disability field. He contrasted our rates to those of Scandinavian countries, because those countries had better prenatal and postnatal services. An initial scan of the speeches reveals several themes, the most prominent being that *given our wealth, it is our responsibility as a country to do better*. These themes reflected the desire by families who had a child with a disability for interconnectedness to a greater society that was committed to supporting them and to correcting the wrongs done, and not only for disabled American people, but to take these steps forward as global leaders.

One would have expected that noted speechwriter Ted Sorenson composed these words; however, in a 1994 interview, Eunice Kennedy Shriver states that neither she nor Sorenson wrote these references to persons with mental retardation. This further enhances the commitment from a personal level of one leader's attempt to forward the movement. Despite the valiant efforts of the first President Bush in enacting the Americans with Disabilities Act (1990) that took further strides toward making persons with disabilities fully included citizens, little progress has been made since. JFK's approach was successful because it was not solely a top–down approach; it encouraged activism from the grassroots.

While complexity theory was not a prominent social science research paradigm in the 1960s, JFK and his supporters did consider the initial conditions of persons with disabilities and the overall situation of these individuals and their families. This provided an attraction for those interested in the movement by first defining common and attainable goals—reducing the incidence of intellectual and developmental disability—and then becoming international leaders. His legacy created and used feedback in developing a system to inform parents and researchers by implementing a science-to-service approach. This lead to self-organization by consumers of the services and an emergent behavior in the form of decentralized disability services. It then accelerated the closure of institutions and the shift to community services. So, based on these strides, what are the next steps for the new leadership? Will they include increased federal funding for supported employment, self-determination, and micro-enterprises? Are there new initiatives to encourage and assure the full participation and citizenship of persons with intellectual and developmental disabilities? Certainly, from the available media, the current candidates have stated little.

Social innovations, within both the public and private sectors, reflected broad and deep attempts to address the complex issues related to disability. Such social innovations (to be discussed in chapter 8) occur in multiple settings through self-organizing from the grassroots. In the United States, social change typically happens incrementally. On rare occasion when conditions allow for a significant change, as occurred in the Kennedy years, we must embrace these changes—and now we must question who will take the disability rights movement to the next stage.

EXAMPLE 2: A COMPLEX SYSTEMS APPROACH TO ORGANIZATIONAL ACCREDITATION

This project used a complex systems (complexity) approach to program evaluation as a vehicle for a social service organization providing employment support services to persons with intellectual disabilities to meet their CARF accreditation standards (CARF, 2010). It further reviews complexity and links the use of social networks as a nonlinear approach to outcomes. This application approaches the issue from a social and economic justice viewpoint, given that society reflects the technology available to it. Those without access are at a social disadvantage. Persons served (agents) need access to information technology for connecting (e.g., employment applications, establishing contact with family). Input of persons served relates to grassroots organizing.

The CARF approach has its roots in the cybernetics-based quality improvement movement wherein, since the late 1940s, various industries seek to improve their processes and quality. The benefits of CARF accreditation lie in its monitoring approach to employment and community supports, rehabilitation, and behavioral health programming. Characteristics of the CARF accreditation process include that it is person-centered; that it is consultative rather than inspective; that it accredits programs, not organizations; that it follows practices consistent with participatory program evaluation practice; that it encourages use of evidence-based practices; and that it uses persons internal to the organization (including consumers) to monitor and improve services.

Similar to other accrediting bodies in the health and social services sector, CARF applies a peer-review process with standards emerging from field practitioners and executives. Specific benefits of accreditation include an increased understanding of program operations by key stakeholders at all levels; relevant and timely feedback; reduced organizational risk; increased practitioner professionalism; an internally driven approach; a similarity to action research; encouragement to improve services through staff cooperation; integration into the programs' daily operations and systems; ongoing feedback for improvement purposes; and improved client satisfaction.

A method was needed for a cohesive approach for understanding how an organization emerges, what attracts clients (agents), how these agents self-organize, how the system uses feedback, and how an emergent behavior results. Differential program evaluation, developed by Tripodi, Fellin, and Epstein (1978), fit the bill, as it used multiple approaches to understand varying outcomes for several evaluation and monitoring activities.

We approached this study from a complex systems perspective. Complex systems, or complexity theory, seeks to identify an underlying order to apparently disordered phenomenon by using agent-based (client) modeling to discern choices that leads to an emergent behavior or pattern. The components of complexity include that it is agent-based, that it has heterogeneous options, that it has attractors, that it is self-organizing, and that it results in an emergent behavior. This theoretical approach, given social work's person-in-environment perspective, has potential applications in consumer and organizational decision making, planning, and outcomes management.

We focused on the *attractor* concept of complexity theory in order to encourage successful treatment. Substance abuse programs benefit by identifying and providing attractors that lead to successful completion. These attractors—forces that lead to clients grouping together in order to improve likelihood of success—fit within a complexity approach and lead to a desirable and emergent group behavior (Johnson, 2002; Wolf-Branigin, 2006).

Self-organization, as a concept applied by social service planners and evaluators, relies on general systems theory to identify and understand consumer choices (Wheatley, 1999; Proehl, 2001). While this framework provides a model for understanding these interactions, it has a limited ability to quantify emergent and iterative changes. As an alternative, Patton (2002) suggests that complexity theory provides a promising framework for shaping and structuring the information collected when planning for these interventions. This provides an overview of these components and their application as second-order cybernetics or sociocybernetics (Felix-Geyer & van der Zouwen, 2001) whereby the initial feedback serves as the basis for a social constructivist analysis.

EXAMPLE 3: EDUCATION—COLLABORATIVE LEARNING ON THE ADA

This study applied the concepts of using diverse perspectives and heuristics for educating social work students about the Americans with Disabilities Act of 1990 (ADA) through collaborative learning. Collaborative learning, based on Vygotsky's (1978) zone of proximal development, provided the framework for an assignment whereby our bachelor of social work (BSW) students, with disabilities and without, gained insight into their surrounding physical environment. This zone-of-proximity development process follows a framework where joint efforts on behalf of students and instructors coalesce into learning.

Interactions between peers within this framework are viewed as an effective means of developing skills and strategies using cooperative learning exercises, where students with less knowledge of the topic are paired with students with a greater level of knowledge within this zone of proximal development. Within the learning situation, the benefits of the student's diverse perspectives and problem-solving approaches—the heuristics—create an environment facilitating creative thought, application, and problem solving (Page, 2007).

To acquaint BSW students with the issues that persons with disabilities encounter routinely, they worked in pairs to search for understanding, meaning, and solutions, or to create a product of their learning. The task focused on provisions found in the Americans with Disabilities Act (1990). The assignment was designed so that students would apply digital imaging technology to identify an environmental barrier, and then digitally remove or alleviate the identified barrier using *Adobe Photoshop Elements* software. The objectives for the assignment were for BSW students in a junior-year social policy and social justice course to critically assess the physical environment, learn about Americans with Disabilities Act (ADA), become familiar with the standards of the ADA, use image manipulation software, and propose a resolution to an identified environmental barrier.

Based on this experience, the learning outcomes for the participating junior-year BSW students yielded several promising results. First, all student groups successfully completed the assignment; all pairs collaborated and contributed their skill sets to others in their groups; students acquired underlying knowledge of ADA standards as measured through CSWE program assessment standards; and students applied these standards to problem solving.

Social workers are often late in adopting innovation. However, as prospective and practicing social workers, our stakeholders expect that we develop and participate in a implementing various information technologies to enhance the students' educational experience. This need led representatives of our department to consider electronic alternatives from two perspectives. The first, involved creating robust social networks that can accommodate a variety of threats to their existence. The second approach involved the resilient use of prospective users of this technology. New media tools (e.g., wikis, mash-ups, and social networking) provide promising platforms for social service communities to self-organize, problem solve, and facilitate multidisciplinary collaboration (Hollingshead & Contractor, 2006). The anticipated benefits include encouraging collaboration with colleagues on promising practices; organizing and facilitating social action in the form of advocacy; applying new information technology to a highly interactive profession; and encouraging good practice vis-à-vis developing social networks.

In preparing professional social workers, we set four student-centered objectives:

1. To demonstrate oral and written communication skills and critical thinking commensurate with beginning-level professional expectations
2. To work collaboratively within the purpose, structure, and functions of organizations as systems
3. To demonstrate the ability to use information technology to communicate, conduct research, and expand the knowledge within an ethical context
4. To identify personal, societal, and professional value systems and their relationships to intervention strategies.

This initial foray revealed the ability to expand the tasks to other faculty and across both our bachelors' and masters' programs. Additionally, the focus shifted from being invasive (faculty or course centered blogs) to becoming student-centered (collaborative and active).

EXAMPLE 4: COMMUNITY NEEDS: TRAVEL TRAINING

Travel training services illustrate one example of encouraging livable communities through accessibility. Transportation providers, who are typically public transit agencies, agree that solutions must be identified to curb the high cost of specialized services to people with disabilities. Simultaneously avoiding costly paratransit services and increasing independence and mobility of people with disabilities through travel training services provides all with a mutual win. In bridging this need for sustaining livable communities, and measuring the efficiency of travel training services, we designed (1) a budget template with line item expenses; (2) a formula to ascertain distinct travel training costs; and (3) an examination of the benefits of travel training services to trainees, to the community, and to public transportation providers (funders) to ascertain whether travel training saved or diverted costs.

In the past decade, as resources for providing paratransit services for persons with disabilities have tightened because of governmental deficits, the need for and benefits of teaching individuals with disabilities how to use public transportation has become more apparent. Social service and transportation professionals began devoting resources to design and implement travel training services to assist individuals shift from the paratransit system to fixed route systems, such as buses. Travel training programs provide instruction in travel skills to individuals with any disability except visual impairment (Groce, 1996). This inquiry into the emergence of travel training studied four properties of organizations or systems: intention, boundaries, resources, and exchange, as suggested by Katz and Gartner (1988). These properties were used to facilitate information sharing among the participating organization.

As travel training commenced for people with disabilities to use fixed route transit and increase their independence, benefits became apparent for the trainers, too, in creating a professional association to strengthen their efforts in refining pedagogy, discussing funding streams, communicating information about administrative and human resource policy and practice, developing mechanisms to inform themselves, and sharing promising and best practices. Travel training evolved to meet the emerging needs of persons using paratransit and other transportation services, as well as for those involved in helping them.

Such instruction provided an innovative strategy for increasing ridership for various populations including persons with intellectual and developmental disabilities (Crain & Associates, 1998). Furthermore, it has become popular to demonstrate to older adults how to increase their independence by using public transportation (Burkardt, McGavock, & Nelson, 2002). Representatives of public transit agencies state that having persons with disabilities use conventional transit provides a cost-effective alternative. Achieving this required that conventional transit become more accessible (Iannuzziello, 2001).

Easter Seals Project ACTION (ESPA) is a national training and technical assistance center for accessible transportation that was commissioned by the U.S. Congress in 1988 as a national research and demonstration project. While each travel training service is unique, the major activities typically include a comprehensive set of services, such as assessment; trip planning; familiarity of the built environment; travel instruction plan development; and strategies of instruction. These strategies focus on crossing streets, using public conveyor systems, boarding, riding, alighting vehicles, and handling emergencies (ESPA, 2007).

This study addressed three areas of interest to advocates of travel training service. First, attempt to quantify the current practices, capacities and outputs of travel trainers employed by transit authorities and agencies. Second, identify the initial trends in order to inform travel trainers and organizations attempting to improve their services. Finally, propose an evaluation and research agenda to enhance further the travel training profession. We applied a systems evaluation framework focusing on the three waves of systems theory: general systems theory, cybernetics, and complexity science (Midgley, 2006). General systems theory encourages stakeholders to consider the three levels of systems involved in a person's life. First the micro level (e.g., family and friends), second the mezzo level, involving local organizations providing services, and finally the macro level, involving federal and state policy that affects the provision of services.

Applying a cost–benefit model to travel training appears to measure improvements in community livability for people with disabilities, assist public transportation providers improve their decision making, save public transportation providers financial resources, and contribute to the sustainability of local transportation systems. Given the assumption that the public transportation provider (funder) will garner the lowest benefit–cost ratio, compared to the trainee and community, these findings suggest that travel training services provide an effective and efficient alternative for public transportation providers seeking to reduce or avoid paratransit costs. Public transportation providers should require that those delivering travel training services submit the necessary information in order to improve decision making, analyze the data from internal or contract personnel, and use the results as a decision tool and a rationale to expand travel training services. If cost savings are derived, they should share knowledge about the benefits of travel training services with other public transportation providers.

Travel training can be viewed in this situation as a win–win. Both the public transportation system and the persons with disabilities improved their situation by reducing expenses for the funder and increasing mobility and community access for individual with disabilities (agents).

As we can see, social service and other organizations are often in the situation where their decisions are made based on flawed or incomplete information. Such flaws include limited information, samples and responses gathered within a short time frame, or samples not representative of their intended populations. Besides these flaws, organizations may also fail to inquire about effects over time. Many need assessments also use data from the decennial US Census, local United Way assessments, or regional health planning bodies. As a result, current needs assessment approaches frequently contain arbitrary boundaries and static or cross-sectional data collection methods. Needs assessments answer questions about the social conditions a human service intends to address and the need for a social service program, and they determine whether the need for a new program exists. These methods may compare or prioritize needs within a program area or across various program areas (Rossi, Lipsey, & Freeman, 2004).

Accurately estimating need remains difficult but, nevertheless, it is important, because social problems that are inappropriately defined are susceptible to several potential problems, including programs that continue to conduct the same activities and not implement new approaches, or entities that simply respond to a necessary condition for the sake of the funding and/or accreditation. In many instances, forces exist within organizations and by professions to limit change and innovative solutions.

EXAMPLE 5: HOUSING PATTERNS

In this example autocorrelation was applied in two ways: using a geographical spatial autocorrelation approach, and through a k-means clustering. Exploratory and interactive spatial analysis often relies on an inductive approach rather than deductive hypothesis-testing. This evaluation used spatial analysis to measure community inclusion.

Community inclusion of people with intellectual and developmental disabilities assumes that all individuals have the right to be fully participating citizens of their communities. This shift is represented by changes in employment, housing, and educational policies, as well as other services affecting people with disabilities. This study supports the further use of spatial point pattern analysis as a promising method for measuring the degree to which people with developmental disabilities are physically included in their communities. The issues discussed do not purport to assess the degree that people interact with others, only the degree to which people were dispersed geographically throughout their community.

As discerned through spatial autocorrelation procedures, the number of people residing in the home did not lead to clustering. The utility of measuring autocorrelation may best be viewed in a context where the movement of people with disabilities over the past three decades from institutional to community residences may be viewed in a manner similar to an ethnic group becoming assimilated into a region. Because of this lack of autocorrelation, people with disabilities appeared to have been successfully geographically included. These expectations were based on two assumptions. First, the more included the person in the community, the more likely the individual would be residing with fewer people who had disabilities. The second expectation was based on the assumption that the more included the person was in the community, the more likely that individual would have people (allies and supporters) who took an interest in him or her. These people would, therefore, attend important life-planning functions.

The presence of friends and family members at the individual's planning meeting should be viewed with caution. Although this indicator has the potential of predicting inclusion in a person's community, person-centered planning methods are relatively new and have not been totally integrated into the operations of organizations providing services. People with disabilities frequently had several family members present at their meetings, regardless of their level of disability, earned income, or type of home in which they resided. This may be further explained by the possibility that those individuals with the most severe disability had similar levels of familial attendance as did people with less severe disabilities. As individuals increasingly controlled more of the services they received, they appeared to rely more on feedback from their friends and family members. This interaction with others outside the service network appeared to create housing options and promote housing patterns that appear random.

Spatial dependencies often are represented as clusters. Assessing spatial autocorrelation, the extent to which the occurrence of an event in one area (housing) is influenced by the distribution of similar features of a neighboring area, is one method for understanding these dependencies. Using spatial autocorrelation, the objective was to determine whether housing patterns were clustered or nearing randomness. Although similar applications of spatial autocorrelation have been applied to other fields, such methods had not been used to measure community inclusion. The objective was to find an absence of clustering or autocorrelation.

A common statistic measuring spatial autocorrelation, Moran's I (Cressie, 1993), resembles a Pearson product-moment correlation coefficient. When a k-means cluster analysis was performed on the same data, similar results occurred. The agents (represented as persons with a disability), who were living independently, resided in the more densely populated portions of the region. Their choice of housing options tended to occur closer to transit lines so that they could travel more freely to their employment, educational, and other environments. The cluster analyses, representing the emergent pattern, demonstrated that larger homes had greater mean distances from their respective group centroid (the mean location within a cluster). These greater distances potentially indicate more isolation from the community at large. This was especially true for the three and four person homes.

This dispersion likely occurred because larger homes had their own transportation and therefore could be located farther from public transportation that could be found in the more densely populated areas. Group centroids likewise indicated that all people who were living independently resided in the more densely populated areas. The feedback component (defined as having more established support systems), represented itself by the number of family members and nonprofessional staff at the clients' planning meetings. Simple rules (boundaries), as represented by a county ordinance requiring that group homes be located at least 500 feet apart from each other, possibly played a role in the housing pattern. As analyses using similar approaches occur, evaluators and researchers need to attend to similar simple rules.

While this may appear contrary to the hypothesis, homes with more unrelated persons living in them might have had financial resources allowing for greater dispersion. Placement of homes likewise may have resulted from zoning issues that led to larger residences being located in less populated areas. People living alone or with fewer unrelated persons appear to benefit from residing in more populated areas of the region. This may have reduced the likelihood of being more physically dispersed but having more random dispersion patterns. This finding suggests that the more included the person is in the community, the more likely that individual would have allies and supporters who take an interest and who would attend important life planning functions.

Complexity provides a promising tool for organizations created to increase community inclusion. Development of these models may include approaches such as empirical and hierarchical Bayesian methods, because of their probabilistic nature, and to a lesser extent small area estimation. An additional and possibly integral interest includes the use of appropriate robust statistical methods for organizational decision making. This issue again remains vital in applications related to disabilities and behavioral health where relatively small samples are available.

The complexity concept of conflict and cooperation arose in this example. In the 1970s, as the organization shifted its focus from being an institution to community inclusion, parents of the clients, their advocates, and organization administrators created community-based living opportunities, including independent living, semi-independent living, and group homes. While independent living is the preferred option, during the time of the deinstitutionalization movement, group homes were viewed as significant progress toward having persons with disabilities live in communities. Residents in the communities, however, initially were not eager to have individuals with disabilities reside in their neighborhoods. Zoning restrictions were put into effect by local governments to assure that a new group home could not be within 500 feet of an existing group home. This initial conflict over limiting group home placement had a long-term positive effect on all parties because it eliminated the likelihood that too many homes would be located in the same neighborhood, thus creating a cluster of group homes. Such a cluster would, in effect, be contrary to the desire of having individuals living in the group homes included in their local communities.

As social work researchers adopt spatial and complexity approaches, rigorous methods including simulation models will provide new insights into social service functioning. The next chapter introduces agent-based modeling (ABM) and provides the initial tools for creating a simulation example that applies the complexity paradigm more rigorously.

APPLICATION OF COMPLEXITY CONCEPTS

In the preceding examples we envision how the components and related concepts of complexity theory can be applied to multiple social work research and evaluation situations. Related concepts include strengthening of social support networks, use of conflict and cooperation, diverse perspectives, and diverse heuristics for solving problems (see Figure 5.1). In the historical analysis, conflict and cooperation were exhibited in the paradigm shift from institutional to community-based services. Similar conflict and cooperation was seen in the studies evaluating travel training, because some persons preferred their current paratransit service. It was also present in the study of housing patterns of persons with disabilities, because neighbors to the group homes were initially apprehensive.

The edge of chaos was demonstrated in the historical study and organizational accreditation. In the historical analysis, an instability in service provision occurred during the systems change, while in the accreditation example organizational learning facilitated internal systems change within the organization in order to conform to standards. Diverse heuristics for problem solving occurred in the educational collaborative learning study, as students used the diverse perspectives of persons with disabilities to gain insight. Robustness similarly played a large role in the travel training study as transit agencies needed to become more sustainable and resilient to economic conditions. The lower costs of travel training supported this objective.

In chapter 6, methods for building simulations within an agent-based environment are introduced. These models can be built using traditional research methods, and then tested under varying assumptions. Using this information, two models are developed in chapter 7. Granted, the models built through ABM may be a bit more rigorous, but envisioning this method as a computer game, such as the SimCity Societies (Electronic Arts, 2007), provides a useful way for approaching the subject. In essence, we seek to build an artificial society that represents the social work issues under inquiry (Epstein, 2006; Mäyrä, 2008). These issues revolve around individual and family decisions and behaviors that lead to a larger emergent behavior of the entire generated society. ABM bridges narrative and quantitative methods, it's explicitly contextual, and it better addresses the need of program personnel for both current and future focused data. This widely applicable framework aids in better understanding ecological and social phenomenon embedded in complex dynamic systems

Evaluation Example	Complexity Component(s)	How Applied
Historical/policy analysis: disability services	1. Conflict–Cooperation 2. Bordering between chaos and equilibrium	1. Change from institutional to community approach 2. Instability in systems during change
Organizational: Accreditation	1. Bordering between Chaos and Equilibrium 2. Scalability	1. Organizational learning occurring during preparation 2. Evaluation tools can be applied as services expand
Educational: Collaborative learning	1. Diverse Perspectives 2. Diverse heuristics for problem-solving	1. Students bring different insights and experiences 2. Integration of different insights and experiences
Community need: Travel training	1. Conflict/Cooperation 2. Robustness and Resiliency	1. Some transportation customers prefer paratransit 2. Fixed route transportation more reliable
Housing patterns	1. Conflict–cooperation 2. Scalability	1. Some neighbors and family members resistant to change 2. Housing model can be replicated at smaller cost

Figure 5.1 Complexity Concepts and Applications in Selected Social Work Evaluations.

SUMMARY

This chapter reviewed several applications that used complexity theory as a guiding framework for conducting social program evaluations. It then sought to clarify further how several of the concepts related to complex systems were applied. The next chapter introduces the reader to the task of developing an ABM. The chapter discusses cellular automata, the successive generation from the agents' actions that simulate or generate what we expect to observe in the model, and serves as an entry to understanding ABMs. Contrary to reductionist research approaches that impose top–down modeling to understand individual and aggregate client behavior, ABM provides a method that accounts for individual behavior and integrates this information to allow for the collective effects of individual responses to social interventions.

EXERCISE

Simple rules play a vital role in assessing complex systems. As an undergraduate psychology major, one influence of mine was the Premack Principle (Malott, 1973), which in effect states that organisms tend to do activities they like and avoid those they do not like. In a philosophy of social sciences class we studied the battle between determinism and free will by applying Einstein's quantum mechanics and the unpredictable randomness that occurs. As an exercise, identify theoretical influences from earlier coursework from your undergraduate or graduate education and analyze how these fit into a complex systems approach.

6

Introduction to Agent-Based Modeling

Agent-based modeling (ABM) provides a viable approach for investigating complex phenomena. ABM computationally simulates the interactions of autonomous agents in order to assess their effect on whole systems and aids in visualizing that clients self-organize at the grassroots level. ABMs create a "social reality" generated from several inputs. This chapter provides the reader with essential background in developing an ABM, including downloading and installing the freely distributed NetLogo software, and using the tab features to write, debug, and run code. Although more advanced software is available, NetLogo software has the advantage of being user-friendly, as it evolved from StarLogo, a software package developed to introduce elementary school students to computer modeling. Computational models are computer programs that we develop. Yes, we as social workers can do this, and this chapter provides the basics for accomplishing this.

This chapter was developed in the spring of 2011 using the most current version of NetLogo software. As the software is updated at least annually, the screen shots and other materials may not exactly match the latest version that you download. But the developers of NetLogo usually attempt to make newer versions compatible with earlier ones.

Learning objectives for this chapter include

- becoming familiar with the logic of agent-based modeling (ABM);
- understanding how ABM serves as a method to inquire into complex systems;
- becoming familiar with the commands of one ABM program (NetLogo).

ABM simulates the interactions, characteristics, or preferences of individual agents. The appeal for this method is particularly attractive within a complexity approach, because it is this individual-agent or grassroots level that leads to an emergent behavior for the entire group. Whereas computational modeling has been applied in the physical sciences for decades, it is with ABM that we can create models based on the actions and decisions of individuals. Because of these individual level interactions, ABM has relevance to modeling social realities. ABM allows us to visualize the larger patterns resulting from the individual-agent-level interactions. Using information from the worked exercise at the end of chapter 2 ("How Complexity Components Apply to Housing for Persons with Disabilities"), we will apply this material into building a model in chapter 7 that reflects the influence of individual characteristics of these persons with intellectual disabilities and their social interconnectedness. The resulting model will demonstrate how certain influences affect where these individuals live and how they use transportation. As we will see, ABM has particular relevance as a research tool that applies complexity theory because of its use of agent–client level data. This allows for information concerning individual decisions and preferences to be entered into the model-building.

This evaluation used a quantitative geography approach, or spatial analysis, to evaluate the efficacy of community inclusion of 2,300 people who transitioned from institutional residences to community residences, including small group homes, foster homes, and supported/shared living units.[1] The successful inclusion of people with disabilities into the community was in part the result of support by individuals' families and advocates.

Complexity and chaos theory as applied in social work literature has scant application of agent-based modeling. Recent studies, however, have shifted from these conceptual manuscripts to focus increasingly on the metaphorical application to social service populations. The evaluation we discussed in chapter 5 on community inclusion efforts in suburban Detroit for people with intellectual and developmental disabilities, provides one framework for constructing a complexity model of program evaluation. As you will notice, the building blocks for the model came from using traditional research methods for conducting a literature review: formulating a hypothesis, identifying variables, sampling, creating a research design, and measuring the variables.

BACKGROUND OF AGENT-BASED MODELING

Social scientists in recent years have added ABM as a new computational method for understanding actor (agent) and context interactions present in complex and dynamic systems. Recent advances in computational power allow for improvements in modeling this bottom-up approach, in which we can begin to understand the influence of several layers of information (or variables) upon individuals and then model the collective behavior that arises. This framework links qualitative narrative and quantitative modes of inquiry, respects contexts, and addresses current and future data needs.

This model has wide applicability in understanding and forecasting a variety of ecological and social phenomenon embedded in complex dynamic systems (Lewin, 1999). This chapter introduces one version of ABM software and provides a primer on building, running, and interpreting such models. This likely will be a novel approach, not covered in any social coursework, so a degree of patience will aid in comprehending the material.

One scheme for classifying ABMs into three forms (abstract, middle-range, and facsimile models) was proposed by Gilbert (2008). Abstract models demonstrate a basic social process that may underscore social life. Facsimile models attempt to reproduce a specific phenomenon as precisely as possible. Facsimile models are useful when seeking to predict the future state of a phenomenon or when forecasting the effects of a policy change. Middle-range models, which describe characteristics of social phenomena, fall between abstract and facsimile models. In chapter 5, a middle-range model (Travel Training Services) and a facsimile model (Housing Patterns) were developed.

Building ABMs allow researchers to identify decisions rules and context features that are sensitive to variation. Identification of sensitive parameters allows for a better understanding of the fundamental processes at work within a social context and the intended audience for change. This is critical because contexts frequently shift, and resources for change are usually finite, particularly in regards to social welfare and services. As social work research and evaluation demands to produce contextually relevant, robust models of behavior increase, ABM will provide a useful tool for such investigations.

FORECASTING THE COMPLEX: AGENT-BASED MODELING WITH NETLOGO SOFTWARE

Although agent-based modeling has few examples presently in the social work literature (Israel & Wolf-Branigin, 2011), health and social science applications abound. These include public health (Gorman, Mezic, Mezic, & Gruenewald, 2006), racial segregation (Schelling, 1978), behavioral and ecological interactions (Epstein & Axtell, 1996), drug epidemics (Agar, 1999), and evaluation of the social science literature (Epstein, 1999). Early examples of ABM typically are based on game theory, in which an agent attempts to anticipate a competing agent's strategy. This may be seen in the study of competition and cooperation (Axelrod, 1984, 1997) in which agents who cooperate with others tend to gain more long-term benefits than those who prefer conflict.

As it becomes apparent in the example presented, the modeling of complex systems work best with the longitudinal and spatial data sets that are present in social service organizations. Because complexity encourages the use of an iterative process and a priori information contained in management information systems, models created under a complex systems approach generate multidimensional perspectives of social service phenomena. As will be discussed in the final chapter, future efforts to develop complexity applications in social program evaluation may include delineating a concise set of prompts for defining the components of complex systems, and creating viable procedures and a checklist for program planners and evaluators to use.

The advantages and disadvantages of investigating complexity through agent-based modeling are numerous. Among its advantages, is that it builds upon Patton's utilization-focused evaluation (2008). A complexity model best performs when empowered agents select services from program options based on information they receive (Patton, 2011). Additional advances in complex networks (Barabasi, 2002) suggest methods for identifying and increasing the interconnectedness amongst participants in "small world" networks by adding additional linkages to others with similar interests in their communities. We can see a practical example of this in the disabilities field, where in the past few decades a growing interest in developing natural supports for persons with disabilities arose. This use of natural supports, people who become friends or allies of individuals with disabilities and who receive no remuneration, parallels the idea of "small world" networks because, in effect, these natural supports are creating additional community connections for the person with a disability.

In the past five years we have seen social work researchers begin to use ABM. These articles include both conceptual (Woehle, 2007; Israel & Wolf-Branigin, 2011) and social service applications to model social worker turnover and clinical knowledge (Bliss, Gillespie, & Gongaware, 2010), segregation (Jayprakash, Warren, Irwin, & Chen, 2009), and the effects of an intervention on social and cultural capital (Woehle, Jones, Barker, & Piper, 2009). In each of these models, the goal was to identify patterns present in their respective environments rather than to test hypotheses. Based upon these early studies, we may expect many more attempts to use this promising methodology to investigate the layers of data that affect social program evaluation and social work research.

The ability for pattern recognition increases as iterative models that measure emergent trends over time and space become more accessible. They provide an entry into investigating complex social service phenomena. As discussed in chapter 7, ABM was used for a worked example analyzing housing patterns of persons with an intellectual or developmental disability. This computationally intensive simulation approach identified how a set of variables (size of home, presence of earned income, proximity to public transportation, and level of family/advocate support) produced an emergent behavior as measured by spatial autocorrelation. This application focused on the self-organizing that leads to attraction at the micro-level, with progress expected at interpersonal levels rather than macro (systems) level. Using feedback affected several life domains, including housing, education, employment, health, and social services.

ABMs afford the opportunity to observe emergent group behaviors. Such behavior patterns are typically not static, but evolve over time in response to local situations and contingencies. The observation of these behavior patterns and their shifts contrast typical outcome-focused evaluations, where the task is identifying the presence or absence of normative behaviors that produce a single, desired outcome. Although ABMs do not include all of the following characteristics, models typically include the majority of them. Common characteristics include having a finite physical space as plotted on a Cartesian grid, heterogeneous agents with differing preferences, competition for limited resources, resource cost, use of heuristics for resource acquisition, and adaptation over time. A defined two- or three-dimensional space allows researchers to overlay models with features of actual spaces, such as transportation infrastructure, variable costs of movement, and resource distribution. Agent heterogeneity refers to how individual agents vary regarding the vital characteristics under consideration in the model.

The competition for limited funding accounts for the belief that within communities, resources are rarely distributed in ways that fairly and proportionally meet the needs of all persons (Holland, 1975) To account for uneven resource distribution, you can use their current resources to access or leverage additional ones. Resource costs might simply be the energy expended to move to a locale with more resources, or in a more complicated example, a series of exchanges resulting in the acquisition of a resource. Agents are assumed to have finite resources that are expended in an attempt to gain additional resources. Heuristics for resource acquisition refer to the agents' frequent use of simple rules when deciding to act. Adaption refers to the agents adjusting as local conditions change. Failure to adapt leads to loss of resources or not surviving.

Despite the promise of ABMs, such models require explicit rationales for all key parameters. Parameters in these models may have unknown quantities, the assumptions of modelers must be explicit in this work, and estimating parameters must be transparent so that another modeler can replicate a given model and observe the similar behavior patterns found in the original model.

First, a little background regarding cellular automata is useful. This concept consists of a regular grid of cells, each in one of a finite number of options, typically binary, such as "On" and "Off." The grid can be in any finite number of dimensions. For each cell, a set of cells called its neighborhood (usually including the cell itself) is defined relative to the specified cell. For example, the neighborhood of a cell might be defined as the set of cells a distance of 2 or less from the cell. At baseline (time t = 0) is selected by assigning a state (on/off) for each cell. A new generation is created (advancing t by 1), based on a fixed to determine the new state of each cell.

This chapter uses the ABM software NetLogo as the principal means of modeling, but what pieces are really needed to develop such simulations? For the answer, it is useful to apply the same similar sampling and data collection methods discussed in a typical social work research text, and then orient toward the method provided by Gilbert (2008). More advanced researchers wanting to create ABMs and to simulate interactions given the existing longitudinal data sets should consider using the Multi-Agent Simulator of Neighborhoods (MASON, 2010) software. This freely distributed software program simulates multi-agent complex systems. Some advanced computational and programming skills would be useful, because these programs require a basic knowledge of computer modeling. Technical support and tutorials are available from their websites.

DOWNLOADING NETLOGO SOFTWARE

To begin your inquiry into building and analyzing ABMs, it is best to simply download the NetLogo software. NetLogo operates on a series of simple commands or procedures provided to the program by the user. Below are the steps to download, set up and run a model on NetLogo.

1. Download NetLogo 4.1 from the NetLogo site (http://ccl.northwestern.edu/netlogo/download.shtml).

    1.1. After downloading NetLogo 4.1 to your computer, install NetLogo 4.1 on your computer.

2. Open NetLogo 4.1.

    2.1. NetLogo 4.1 will open to the INTERFACE tab. Next to the INTERFACE tab is the INFORMATION tab and the PROCEDURES tab.

    2.2. Note that the INTERFACE tab allows the user to run and observe the simulation.

    2.3. Note that the INFORMATION tab is used by the model's creator to explain the model to other users.

2.4. Note that the PROCEDURES tab is where the user inputs code that creates and runs models.
3. To view the user's manual and receive tutorials on how to operate NetLogo 4.1 go to NetLogo Web-based User's Manual (http://ccl.northwestern.edu/netlogo//netlogo/docs/).
   3.1. Locate a list of different resources, including tutorials listed 1–3, on the left side of the user's manual.
   3.2. Read tutorial 1; it explains how to use models.
   3.3. Read tutorial 2; it explains how to use commands in the INTERFACE tab.
   3.4. Read tutorial 3; it explains how to input procedures in the PROCEDURES tab.
   3.5. Find the NetLogo dictionary below the tutorials in the resources section. The dictionary provides explanations for all NetLogo procedures and it is useful in understanding how to properly use procedures.
4. Return to the open NetLogo 4.1 program on your computer.
   4.1. Select FILE on the top left corner of the screen.
   4.2. Under FILE, select MODELS LIBRARY.
   4.3. Open any of the folders and select a model by double clicking on its name. Several folders will appear with names such as Biology, Social Science, and the like.
   4.4. Adjust any sliding buttons, and run the model to see the types of variables it tests once the model is loaded.
   4.5. Select the INFORMATION tab for an explanation of the model, what it tests, and how it operates. The user can also select the PROCEDURES tab to see the procedures used to create the model. At the bottom of the PROCEDURES tab is the copyright for the code.
   4.6. Find CODE EXAMPLES in the MODELS LIBRARY (second to last folder). The contents provide code examples that are free to be used, altered, or distributed for any legal purpose. These examples outline basic procedures a user may wish to use.
5. Practice using NetLogo by returning to the original untitled model that first appeared when NetLogo was opened.

6. Use the white section of the INTERFACE tab to place buttons that will operate the model and manipulate variables. The black window allows the user to view the model as it runs.

   6.1. To edit, delete, and add new buttons to the interface, use the buttons from left to right on the INTERFACE tab.
   6.2. Add new buttons by clicking on the button labeled BUTTON. A menu will drop down and you can choose any of the buttons that meet the need for the program.
   6.3. Select a button with a left click on the white section of the interface. Once a button is created, a command box will appear that asks you to input the command. For most buttons to function, they must be linked to a procedure in the PROCEDURES tab or be given a command. An example would be to create a button to set up the model. The word SETUP would be typed in the button's command box. This will link the button to the setup procedure and set up the model when pushed. (Note: The forever box in the button's command window allows the procedure that is linked to the button to run continuously.)
   6.4. Note other objects of importance on the top of the INTERFACE tab: the SPEED SLIDER that allows the user to control the speed of the model; the VIEW AND UPDATE boxes that allow the user to choose whether to watch the model as it runs or only to view updates of the model, and the SETTING button that allows the user to make changes to the size and characteristics of the viewer.
   6.5. Use the VIEWER in the black box in the interface. It is also referred to as THE WORLD in NetLogo 4.1. It is made up of patches and laid out as a grid with the center coordinates being 0,0. Unless instructed otherwise in the settings section, THE WORLD will wrap around, meaning that an agent can leave the model on one side and then appear on the other.
   6.6. Find the word TICK with a number beside it in the upper left corner of the VIEWER. This allows the user to count the number of iterations that occur. To count iterations, the command TICK needs to be entered in the TO GO procedure discussed later (see step 8.3).

6.7. Use the INTERFACE tab at the bottom of the COMMAND CENTER. The COMMAND CENTER allows the user to input commands to turtles and patches that the user does not want to make a permanent part of the model. For example the user may want to see what would happen if all the agents were red. So the observers would type in the COMMAND CENTER *"ask turtles [set color red]"*.

7. Use the INFORMATION tab by clicking on it and then left-clicking on the EDIT button to begin writing any information that is important for using the model. The directions in the INFORMATION tab will guide you in knowing what information goes where.

8. To use the PROCEDURES tab, type in commands from tutorial 3 or from the example listed below.

   8.1. Note when using the PROCEDURES tab that it has four options listed at the top.

       8.1.1. Use the FIND option to allow the user to locate procedures that have already been written.

       8.1.2. Use the CHECK option to check the code to make sure that the program has understood correctly; it will highlight any unclear code. CHECK tells the user what the problem is with the code. (It is possible that CHECK will not catch a problem until the model begins to run; this will result in a run-time error message that will tell the user what the problem is.)

       8.1.3. Use the PROCEDURES button to show the names of all the procedures used to create a model.

       8.1.4. Note that INDENT AUTOMATICALLY formats the procedures to indent as they are being written. This can help with identifying where one procedure ends and another begins.

   8.2. Note when entering procedures that most procedures start with the word "to", and end with the word "end". The exception to this is when creating variables, such as setting up *breeds* of agents, *global* variables and agent specific variables such as *peoples-own*. These procedures are defined in the NetLogo Dictionary.

8.3. Use the *to setup* and *to go* commands. These are the two most important procedures, listing all the procedures that are necessary to setup and then to run the model. Procedures listed under *to setup/to go* must be defined as separate procedures later or the program will not run. Buttons called SETUP and GO must also be defined on the interface.

8.4. Create variables that NetLogo does not know. These variables must either be defined as separate procedures in the PROCEDURES tab or as buttons in the INTERFACE tab.

8.5. Use the code below for the model that tests the effects of access to transportation and community support on the ability of people with disabilities to move around their communities. Please enter this code into the PROCEDURES tab and test out the model.

    8.5.1. Create the button necessary to run the model before entering the code.

    8.5.2. Create *setup* and *go* buttons in the INTERFACE.

    8.5.3. Create SLIDER buttons for *green-setup-energy*, *number-of-houses*, *energy-on-rail-line*, *mobility*, and *living-in-community*.

    8.5.4. Create a SWITCH button for *show-energy?* And *turn-rail-line-on-off*.

    8.5.5. Create a PLOT with the x-axis labeled *time*, the y-axis labeled *totals*, and three different plot pens titled: *people without disabilities*, *people with disabilities*, and *people with disabilities living in community*. Make sure that the plot pens all have different colors.

    8.5.6. Note that these buttons and plots will automatically link the following code as it is entered in the PROCEDURES tab.

BECOMING FAMILIAR WITH NETLOGO SCREENS

Several figures are included in this section to visualize how the screens in NetLogo appear. These screen shots are based on the worked example involving housing patterns of persons with disabilities. The NetLogo

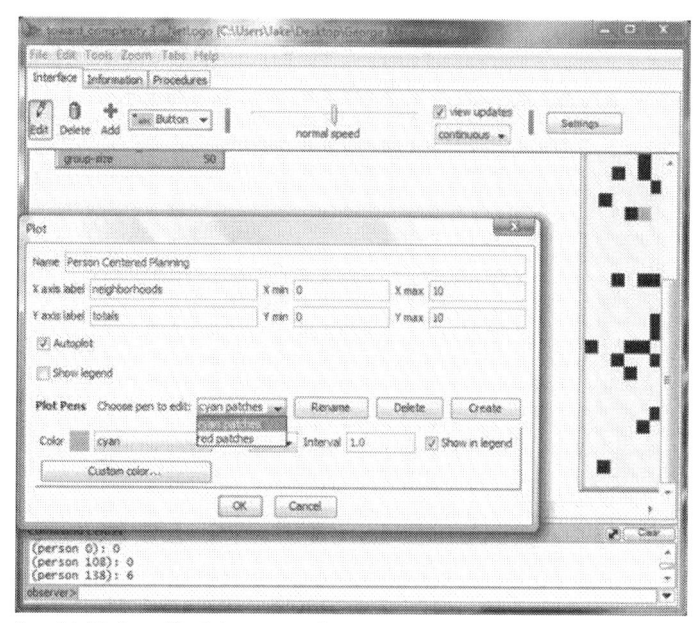

Figure 6.1 NetLogo Blank INTERFACE Screen.

blank interface (Figure 6.1) is the first screen. NetLogo PROCEDURES tab (Figure 6.2) is where the user inputs codes or procedures that create the model, identify the agents in the model, and tell the agents how to behave. At the top of the tab is a toolbar that allows the user to look up procedures that have been written, check that procedures have been written correctly, and automatically indent the procedures as they are written.

The INTERFACE tab (Figure 6.3) allows the user to interact with the model, start and stop the model, and make minor changes to the model. The screen on the right of the interface is a window that allows the user to watch the model as it runs its simulations. The toolbar at the top of the INTERFACE tab is used to create buttons that allow the user to operate the model and make changes to the simulation speed. The INFORMATION tab (Figure 6.4) can be used to explain the model that has been created, so other users can understand how to operate it.

When developing your model, you can use a function to check your procedures and produce error messages. As in Figure 6.5, the CHECK

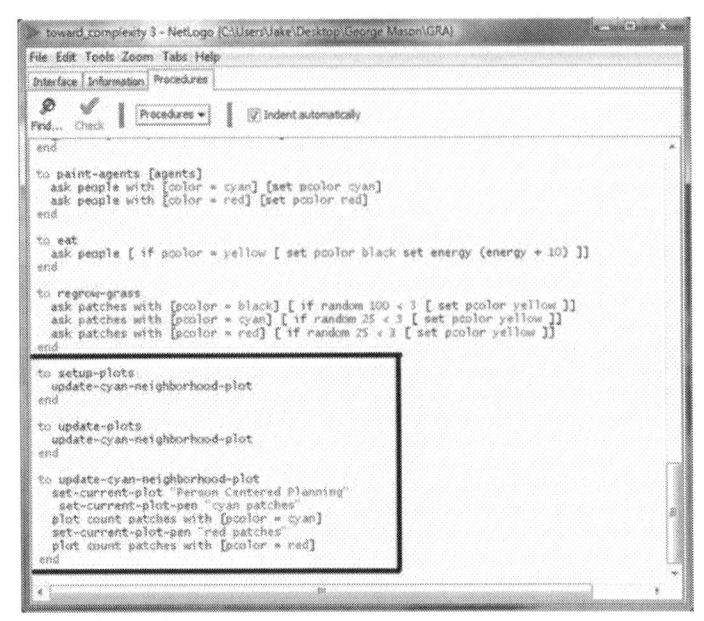

Figure 6.2 NetLogo PROCEDURES tab.

button should be used whenever new procedures are written. Left-click the mouse on the button to use the button. If the procedures were written incorrectly, a box will appear to inform the user that there is an error with the error highlighted. If there are no errors, the CHECK button will change color from green to gray.

Once procedures are entered under the PROCEDURES tab, buttons need to be added to the INTERFACE tab to start, stop, and manipulate the model Figure 6.6 displays how to select buttons on the INTERFACE tab. Left click on either the *"add"* button on the Interface tab toolbar, or on the dropdown menu, and then select the required button.

Once the button is selected, it must be programmed (Figure 6.7). In the picture a SLIDER button has been selected and needs to be programmed. To program this button, the *"global variable"* needs to be defined. The global variable must correspond to the written procedure in the PROCEDURES tab that the user wants to control. The global variable being defined in this button is *"group-size"* which has a corresponding

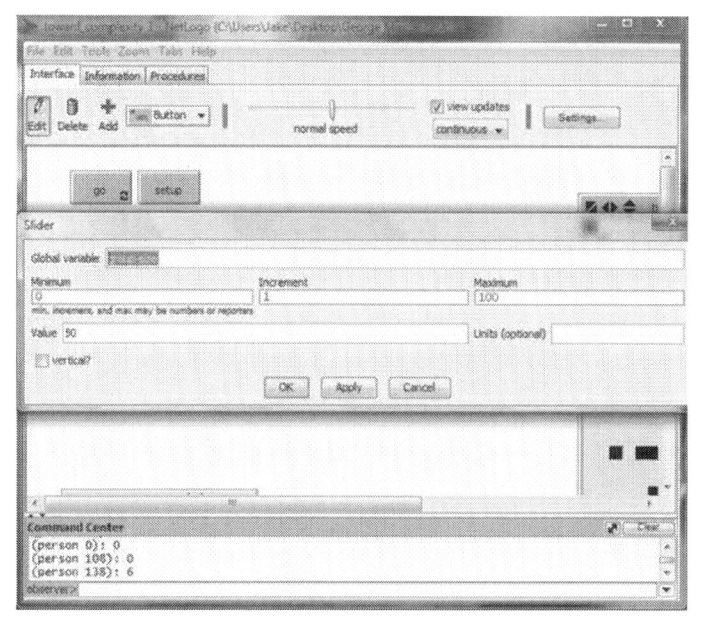

Figure 6.3 NetLogo INTERFACE Tab.

procedure with the same name. The button will allow the user to change the number of groups by sliding the button from 0 to 100. The user can change this range by changing the minimum and maximum numbers as well as the increments.

To create a graph for a model, the following commands need to be given:

"*to setup-plots*"
"*to update-plots*"
Follow with the name of the plot to be updated, such as
  "*update-cyan-neighborhood-plot*"
Then "*to update-cyan-neighborhood-plot*"

Under this command the program is being told that it will be plotting something in the model. The user will need to tell the program (1) what the name of the graph will be—in this case the name is Person

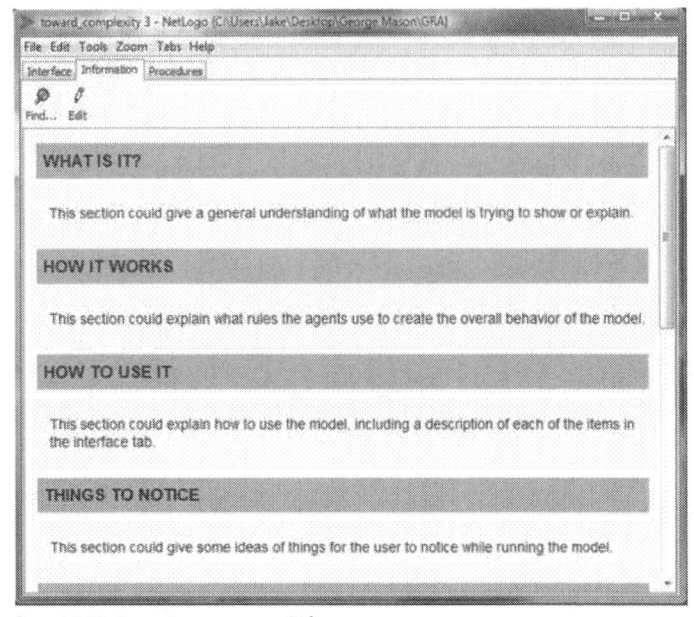

Figure 6.4 NetLogo INFORMATION Tab.

Centered Planning; (2) what is being plotted via the *set-current-plot-pen "cyan patches"* command; (3) how to plot cyan patches via the *plot count patches with [pcolor = cyan]* command. To plot more than one happening in the model, repeat steps 2 and 3, replacing the name *"cyan patches"* or *[pcolor = cyan]* with the name of the item you wish to plot, as was done with plotting the number of red patches.

Having created the graph in the PROCEDURES tab, a graph now needs to be created in the INTERFACE tab. Creating a graph in the INTERFACE is similar to creating and programming a button. The graph must have the same name as in the PROCEDURES: *Person Centered Planning*. The x & y axis need to be named (in this case they are named *"neighborhoods"* and *"totals"*). The pens that will be plotting the changes in the program need to created to match the pen names in the procedures: *cyan patches* and *red patches*, as well as colors to match the pen names.

Once all the procedures are written and buttons are created, the program is ready. The program can be run by pressing the *setup* button that

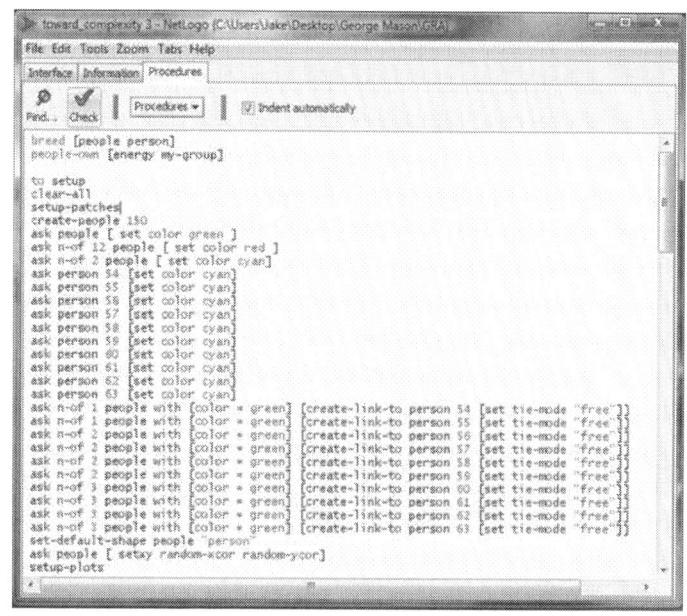

Figure 6.5 How to Use the CHECK button to get PROCEDURE error Messages in NetLogo.

will create the model in the black viewing window. Then select the size of the groups the agents will join, using the *assign-by-size* button, and finally press GO to begin the model (Figure 6.8).

LEARNING THE BASIC NETLOGO COMMANDS

Many of you have already had some experience writing code for a previous class. While writing code may be frustrating, the NetLogo package is relatively simple. The following NetLogo commands are the initial ones that developers of agent-based models should become familiar with.

- *to;* all commands must start with the word *to*. This is the most basic command that tells the model to implement the following command. The *to* command is succeeded by additional

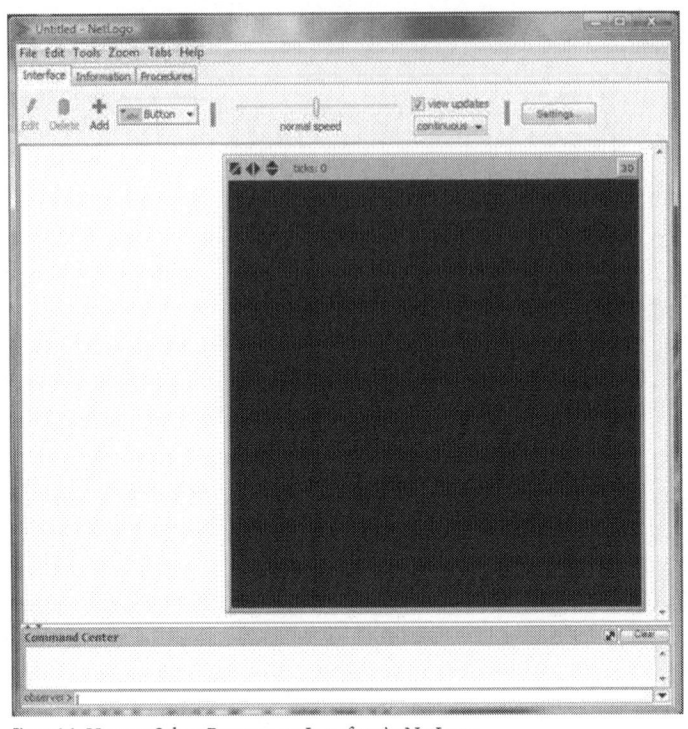

Figure 6.6 How to Select Buttons on Interface in NetLogo.

commands, such as *set, go, assign-by-size, turn-rail-line-on-off,* and so on. Once the *to* command is given, the model can have any number of commands used after that it. Commands can be the traditional, such as those listed here, or they can be impromptu commands created by the code writer. Regardless of where the command comes from, it must start with *to* and be defined in order to work.

- *ask;* this command tells agents and patches to act certain ways in the model. It can ask the agents to move only so many spaces during an iteration, have patches change color in the model, and the like.
- *end;* this command tells the model when the procedure is complete and that no additional commands will be used in that

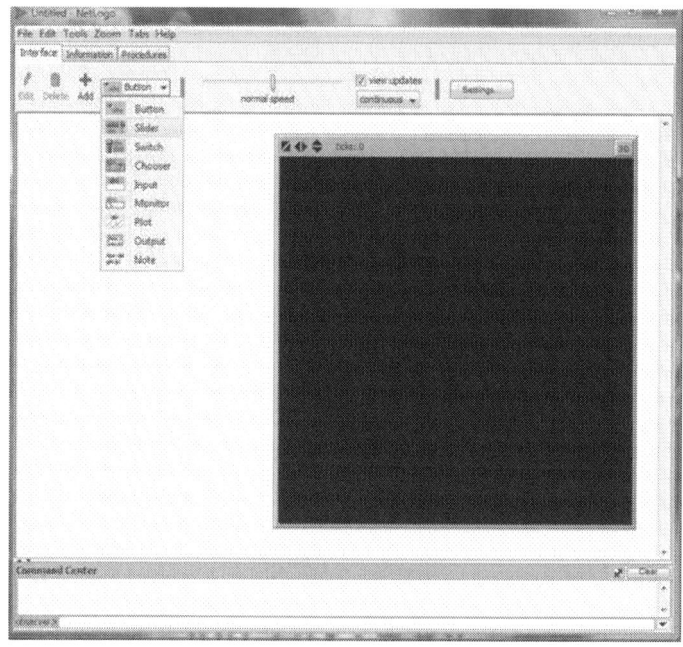

Figure 6.7 Selecting and Programming Buttons in NetLogo.

procedure, similar to how a period signifies the end of a sentence. So every procedure must start with *to* and finish with *end*.

Some other useful commands include:

- *to setup;* this command sets up the model by creating the patches and agents. A corresponding button titled SETUP needs to be created in the interface. Under the *to setup* command, additional information should be provided to define what should be set up.
- *to go;* this commend tells the model to begin to run. Under this command, agents are asked to act out their specific behaviors, and those behaviors are defined using the *ask* command. To go requires a corresponding button in the interface.
- *to eat:* this command uses the *ask* command to have the agents change the color of patches that they are on. This command can be useful for graphing changes in the model.

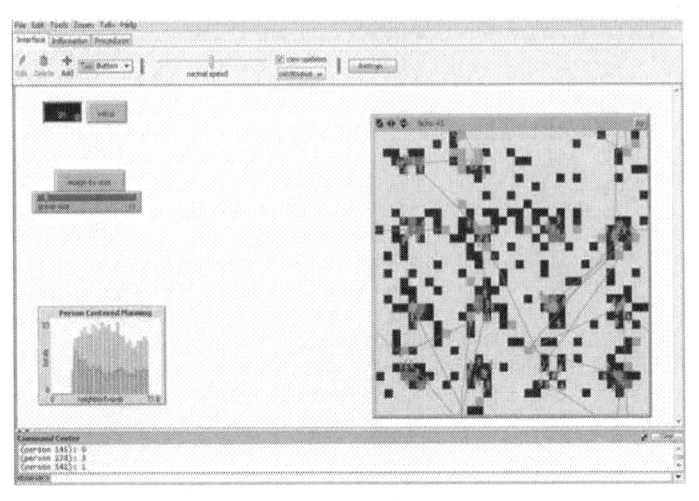

Figure 6.8 How the INTERFACE tab Appears when Running in NetLogo.

- *to regrow-grass*; this command uses the *ask* command to have the patches change their color back to their original color.
- *to die*; this command has agents die if their energy level drops below a certain level. This command can be useful if wanting to track the population of agent groups.
- *To setup-plots*; this command is the first in a series of commands to create plots to track the behaviors of agents and changes in the model. The next line of the command will start with *update-(name of plot)*.
- *to update-plots*; this command tells the model to update the plot and is followed on the next line by the command *update-(name of plot)*.
- *to update-(name of plot)*; this command will specifically tell the model how to update the plot. It will be followed by commands telling the model how to operate the plot with commands *set-current-plot "Name to Appear on Plot"*. The next command will be *set-current-plot pen "pen color"*. This command specifies the color of one the pens for the plot. This command is followed by the command *plot* and then, immediately following this command, the model needs to know what in the model it will be

plotting (e.g., agents or patches of a certain color). Those last two commands should be repeated for every new item that the code writer wishes to have tracked in the plot/graph.

SUMMARY

This chapter introduced an example of agent-based modeling that was developed using input from earlier sections of the book. The following chapter presents social work related models developed using NetLogo software. It further discusses the related methods for assuring that the models you develop are verified and validated. From this initial introduction to the software, you should have gained a beginning level of comfort using modeling software. While the current chapter and those that follow introduce the software, most serious users will need to become more involved in user groups or other supporting materials to obtain answers to the vast array of questions that will arise.

EXERCISE

Open the library in NetLogo and review the available programs. Given your initial introduction, load and run a program. Interpret what the graphs indicate.

7

Developing Agent-Based Models

Building upon the preliminary materials introduced and the skills developed in previous chapters, we now focus on a few models developed for social work related research. Issues related to traditional research methods and their usefulness in developing agent-based models (ABMs) are discussed, and two models will be presented[1]. The first model involves travel training for persons with an intellectual disability. It shows how learning to use public transportation increases the ability to move about the community. The second is a model of housing patterns for persons with intellectual and developmental disabilities. It demonstrates how the housing pattern became randomly distributed as people with disabilities moved from highly segregated institutional patterns to more inclusive community-based housing.

Those planning on developing ABMs are encouraged to review these materials and copy the code into the NetLogo procedures interface to gain an understanding of how the models operate. The output generated from running ABMs is discussed briefly.

The learning objectives for this chapter include

- writing code for agent-based models;
- learning the initial skills to verify and validate these models;

- interpreting and reposting the models.

While many statistical approaches such as social network analysis and k-means cluster analysis are useful in identifying and measuring complex systems, agent-based modeling serves as the most common approach to forecast how complex systems act. Building on the material presented in chapter 6, this chapter reviews two models and the related the code in order to provide social work related examples of ABMs. One useful approach is to create models based on existing quantitative studies, and then change assumptions (e.g., levels of governmental support) to see how the results vary given different conditions or boundaries. Using the forecasting methods in this manner is useful in eliminating the likelihood that the ABMs are solely computerized thought experiments.

THE ROLE OF CELLULAR AUTOMATA

Before developing the models, it is useful to understand the role of cellular automata in ABMs. Cellular automata play an essential role in ABM and spatial autocorrelation, because we are addressing the changes in boxes or cells that result from surrounding influences. This introduces the idea of *lattice data*, which are spatial data where each cell has eight surrounding cells, one immediately above, one immediately below, one to either side, and four on the diagonal. Understanding lattice data plays a prominent role in agent-based models because of how simple rules will affect areas (cells) surrounding the agents.

A benefit of ABM is the ability to isolate specific social variables influencing behavior. This is a central characteristic of cellular automata, the simplification and idealization of a behavior. The challenge in using ABM is determining which variables best fit. The determination of variables can itself be influenced by the capabilities of the ABM software and the suitability of that software to model the social behavior being explored. The profession of social work tends to be systematic in its view of social interactions, seeking to understand how processes at the macro level effect micro level processes and vice versa. Depending on the software used for modeling, a researcher may be able to account for the exchanges from micro to macro, or the researcher may need to assume that outside of the variables being tested all things are equal. That was the assumption of the models constructed with NetLogo.

Models do not consider the effect of external forces on the decisions or behavior of individuals; rather, that knowledge is substituted with the theory of cellular automata. Using cellular automata, the agent operates based on the rules of the model, and those rules act as external regulating forces that are typical in a society. Unlike society, cellular automata treats all agents equally in that the same rules apply to all agents, and all agents move uniformly from one cell to the next. In NetLogo, this equality is represented by each agent having the same degree of mobility. The researcher then identifies the level of inequality wanted in the model and how best to represent that inequality.

PLANNING AN AGENT-BASED MODEL

Framing Your Study as a Complex System

Planning your model begins by using the materials presented in chapter 2. This is the problem formulation stage and involves defining how various aspects fit the components (being agent-based, having an attraction, self-organizing, defining boundaries, using feedback, and creating emergence) of a complex system. Issues, such as reviewing the literature and hypothesis development, will be the similar to the approaches used in traditional research.

Being agent-based builds upon social work's person-in-environment perspective by developing and encouraging the interdependencies of individuals and their environments (Germain & Gitterman, 1980). Modeling a complex adaptive system (CAS) can demonstrate the value of human relationships as a condition to assure that the participant's ecosystem receives a thorough and complete understanding. When developing these models, you must identify the rules under which they will operate, and therefore you are encouraged to revisit the exercise provided at the end of chapter 2. For example, possible evaluation prompts for identifying the agents include, "*Who are the people with whom we are concerned?*" and "*Is the unit of analysis an individual or a group?*"

Attraction in a CAS represents the clients' initial and continued program participation. Attraction is what facilitates an agent's initial interest. It reflects consumer empowerment, and it concerns itself with the complete set of variables affecting client behaviors (Halmi, 2003). Complexity advances the concept of ecosystems by using an open systems approach to explain more than the simple causal explanations to behavior (Bolland & Atherton, 1999). Within social service programs, clients/agents may have different levels of functioning, attributes, and other characteristics when initiating a social intervention. The person's level of functioning affects the type, intensity, and duration of intervention the client receives. For example, within social work's core values, competence and integrity are vital. This assumes that individuals have access to services that address their strengths, preferences, and immediate needs (National Association of Social Workers, 2007). A simple prompt asks, "Why are clients seeking services?"

Self-organization provides the magnet that draws agents together and encourages them to initiate and continue program participation. It identifies how agents or clients with similar interests, strengths, or needs will group together (Hudson, 2000). Examples may include self-help groups or a local neighborhood's efforts to combat gang violence. Building a robust social network in a complex system parallels with the social service concept of resiliency. Through formal and informal networks, self-organizing of agents encourages interdependencies. It promotes dignity and the worth of human relationships by striving to encourage future cooperation, creating network of agents involved in (1) enlarging future impacts, (2) changing the payoffs, (3) teaching people to care about each other, and (4) encouraging reciprocity (Axelrod, 1984). Initial evaluation prompts to consider include, "What is the client's level of functioning when beginning the social service?" and "*What keeps clients motivated to continue or complete services?*"

In social service contexts, boundaries may be defined by legislation, court decisions, or administrative rules supporting policies, funding, or incentives. Boundaries play an essential role in understanding and developing a CAS approach to social program evaluation. For example, Critical Systems Heuristics (Reynolds, 2006; Ulrich, 1996) aids in setting the limits of the evaluation. Boundaries set the limits and define what agents follow that lead to an emergent behavior. A possible prompt asks, "*What rules affect and govern agents' behavior?*"

Feedback informs decision making. Positive feedback includes information from outside the system that can be used to adapt continually to sources of external instability. Negative feedback maintains organizational equilibrium through monitoring or quality assurance and improvement processes (Miller & Page, 2007; Proehl, 2001). Failing to use positive feedback increases the likelihood that an organization maintains the status quo by not responding to new challenges. Organizations that fail to use a wide range of negative feedback affect the dignity and worth of the persons served. This limits consumer empowerment and reduces the possibility of improved service provision by restricting the collective wisdom of the diverse perspectives of current and future clients (Surowiecki, 2004). These organizations self-perpetuate and focus on their own survival by maintaining the status quo. This discourages experimentation and finding new solutions. Evaluation prompts within a complexity framework include, *"Are staff working in partnership with the client in order to use the client's strengths, needs, abilities, and preferences?"* and *"Does the organizational array of services reflect their clients' preferences?"*

Emergent behavior, the final component, represents the outcomes of interventions given the changing context of policy, economic, or cultural conditions. Evaluators using complexity seek to identify nonlinear patterns within outcomes. As conditions change, different patterns may emerge. For example, the movement to community-based services in the 1970s affected the societal desire for persons with intellectual and developmental disabilities to be included increasingly in their communities. To measure this inclusion, we may geographically plot the self-organizing that occurs in housing patterns as individuals with disabilities strive for social inclusion. A random pattern may represent inclusion. When framing the evaluation in a complexity approach, anticipated emergent behaviors may include *"Whether client outcomes reflect any pattern?"* and *"Do client outcomes reflect their strengths, preferences and, abilities?"*

When planning the design of the travel training and housing pattern model, the variables of income, social supports, availability of travel training, incentive for using fixed rail system, and the like were selected as variables because of the primacy of their role in real world scenarios. Planning for the models required identifying how best to represent these variables in the model and how plausible it was to represent these variables. It is possible to have numerous variables represented in the model but the number of variables should be balanced with the programs needed to perform cellular automata. Attempting to test too many variables can lead to a bias in programming that dictates agent behavior instead of creating rules for interaction and this will prevent cellular automata from occurring.

The models featured in this chapter focus on people with disabilities. People with disabilities are represented as having a lower degree of mobility and requiring greater energy expenditure than other agents in the model. These limitations were chosen because mobility was the primary method of interaction in models using cellular automata. The unfortunate side effect of this decision is that it fails to accurately represent the diversity that exists in the disability community. To address this, the observer is able to determine the severity of the limitations but cannot change the nature of it, because it is predetermined by the capabilities of the software.

Selecting Variables

Data that can be best used in developing and informing variable choice for models is numeric demographic information, such as a populations unemployment rate, poverty rate, level of participation in federal assistance programs, length of waiting list for a Medicaid waiver, average number of people in a support system, percentage with a disability, and the like. Data used in developing models for this chapter include proportional representation of people with disabilities in the models. The travel training model includes worksites specifically for people with disabilities that provide compensation far below other worksites. This represents the factor that the nature of a disability can require a person to spend more than they earn just to attend work. The model in the text uses an arbitrary ratio, but a future version of the model could include regionally adjusted income ratios between jobs specifically for people with disabilities and jobs open to everyone.

The housing pattern model was designed to illustrate the multilevel process that people with disabilities go through during deinstitutionalization, and the role a support system can play in the process. This could also be adjusted to more accurately illustrate the number of people in a person's support system or the length of a waiting list for community-based services in a given state. It is best to include geographic information (location), characteristics, and some repeated measures for model building for the purposes of layering variables.

Sampling and Data Analysis

Traditional sampling methods can be used to develop agent-based models. It's best to include all participants in network and spatial analyses, however, because these approaches are typically limited to the actual area or region under study. It may be appropriate to build a sample using qualitative methods, such as snowball sampling and, more specifically, respondent-driven sampling, which builds on snowball sampling by adding mathematical weights to adjust for the fact that the sample was selected in a nonrandom manner. Many ABMs are built on existing studies. We will see this in example 2 later in this chapter, which was built on real data using two previous studies, a spatial analysis study and a k-means cluster analysis. The important aspect is to build ABMs using existing data from other studies if it is either a middle-range or facsimile model.

Verifying and Debugging Models

The purpose of an agent-based model is to identify a behavior occurring at the group level, but many times what appears to be a genuine behavioral phenomenon is instead the result of a programming bug or researcher bias in the way the model was constructed. Verifying the model seeks to assure that it represents what you intend to model, and goes hand in hand with attempting to explain the group behavior being observed in the model. Verifying the model starts with construction of the model. Every procedure written should be checked and tested by running the model. Start with creating a foundation on which the model will operate, and then test the foundation by running the model. If there appears to be no problem in the operation, then move forward with adding additional procedures to the model, checking how each new procedure affects the behavior of agents before moving on to another procedure.

When verifying the completed model, start by running the model multiple times in succession. Carefully observe the outcome of each model and record the results. Slight variation is to be expected in model outcomes. For example, in quantitative research, there can be varying degrees of statistical confidence: 90, 95, or 99, but not 100 percent. Sometimes the model will support the hypothesis, and other times it will not, but if there is no variation in the model outcomes, if the hypothesis is proven or disproven 100 percent of the time, that would indicate that there is a bug in the model. In those instances, the researcher should carefully review the code to determine if a procedure is pushing the outcome in one direction or another. If there is no clear code related error that is causing those outcomes, the researcher should begin to question the validity of the model.

Validating the Model

The process of validating the model is similar to the process of verifying the model, but centers on assuring that the model is consistent with the social reality that it purports to represent. Validating procedures center on the three types of models introduced in Chapter 6; abstract, middle-range, and facsimile.

In abstract models the aim, typically, is to simulate a basic social process. It may be built on deduction. The researcher likely already has a hypothesis concerning agent behavior and the expected emergent behavior to be generated. To begin validation in an abstract model, the researcher assesses whether the model did generate the expected emergent behavior (Gilbert, 2008). To further validate, the researcher may then check what occurs when the model's parameters are varied (based on settings corresponding to the assumptions made) through a sensitivity analysis. The objective is to see whether the emergent behavior or generated pattern changes when the parameters are changed. If the pattern changes, then the researcher needs to identify the condition or change in parameter that leads to the change. To complicate matters, many models have many parameters; therefore it is best to check the output based on all permutations of the change parameters.

In middle-range models, the objective is to describe characteristics of a social phenomenon that can be generalized. Validating these models, therefore, focuses on determining whether the generated models are similar, or have a goodness-of-fit, to the phenomena in the real world (Gilbert, 2008). Middle-range models may generate power laws and represent nonlinear relationships, because the relationships often are log-linear. Validating middle-range models includes both sensitivity analysis and comparisons to empirical data.

Facsimile models are used to forecast what occurs in an intended state or what occurs when a policy or regulation changes (Gilbert, 2008).

The majority of simulations contain a degree of randomness, so exact matches of the initial data and the generated forecast are rare. Validating facsimile models involves comparing a model to empirical data. For a more thorough discussion of validation, please refer to Gilbert (2008). Across all three types of models it is vital to understand that as the models run as a time-series, the values of the output variables change, and this may occur because of autocorrelation.

When observing the agents' behavior, it is important to ask the question, "Is what you are doing necessary?" When creating an ABM with Netlogo, it can be tempting to put too much information into the model in an attempt to include all the variables that would be found in the real world; however, overly constructing the model to meet real world situations can result in agents not being guided by program rules, but rather by observer dictates, and this would invalidate the model's outcomes.

In addressing this concern the researcher should look carefully at the model's design and evaluate it on the following five points:

- Did the researcher start with a simple replication of the variables being tested?
- What are the variables at work in the model and how do they affect each other?
- In attempting to measure the social phenomenon, did the researcher unintentionally incorporate variables into the model?
- What real world variables were not included in the model and why?
- Are the results of the model similar to the results reported in previous studies?

INTRODUCING TWO EXAMPLES

To assist the reader in garnering a better understanding of agent-based modeling, we present two worked examples in this chapter. The first involves a middle-range model of travel training for persons with an intellectual disability and shows that, as the result of learning to use public transit, the ability to move about their community increases for these individuals. In the second example, a facsimile model, we simulate housing patterns for persons with intellectual and developmental disabilities. This model demonstrates that the housing pattern, as it appears, will be distributed within the geographic region in an increasingly random pattern that evolves over time. This occurs because people with disabilities moved from highly segregated institutional patterns to more inclusive community-based housing. The model is further refined to demonstrate how the social connections with friends and family can influence the level of inclusion of people with disabilities in a community. Please note that the coding for the two models are in the appendices and may also be downloaded from the companion website.

Example 1: Travel Training for Persons with Disabilities

This model demonstrates how different factors may influence travel training use by people with disabilities. This model tests the effect of three independent variables on whether people with disabilities will choose to receive travel training to use mass transit. The independent variables are (1) the level of benefit that the person receives from using mass transit, as measured through the amount of energy (also referred to as independence) that the person receives from using mass transit; (2) the level of independence a person has at the beginning of the model; this is also measured using the quantity of energy someone has at the beginning of the model, and (3) the level of work available at any given time during the model.

Work is an integral aspect in allowing someone with a disability to exercise independence. In this model, that ability comes through an increase in energy whenever the person attends work. The dependent variable in this model is based on the number of people with disabilities that choose to receive travel training over a fixed period of time. That is measured through the change in the disability population of red agents (people with disabilities, but without travel training) to black agents (people with a disability and with travel training). There is a third population of people without disabilities (green agents) that compete with the people with disabilities for work.

Energy is the common currency for movement and independence in this model as all agents must have energy to move; however, agents can have a negative energy balance. The rules of the model require that these agents find additional sources of energy, similar to a person with a negative balance in their bank account seeking ways to bring that balance back to a positive number. Energy can be gained by going to work (symbolized by changing the cyan-colored patches to black) or by using mass transit. Although the energy gained is less than energy from employment, using public transit also allows an agent to temporarily increase their movement and receive a temporary energy increase, similar to how someone would be able to rest while riding a train moving 60 miles per hour.

White patches indicate the travel training sites where agents with disabilities can receive training. Additional work could include patches designed for employment services for people with disabilities. The hypothesis of this model is that as the benefit of using mass transit decreases, and as the level of independence for people with disabilities increases, the demand for travel training increases. Appendix A contains the code for example 1. This code can be downloaded from the companion website and then posted into the dialog box in NetLogo. As you can imagine, this model is relatively simple and serves as an introduction to ABMs. The second example will become more evolved and will reflect the use of including a temporal factor into a model.

This model can be adapted to allow the observer greater ability to manipulate variables or to create a model closer to reality. An observer may wish to include procedures that allow for the number of travel training sites to be increased or reduced. This procedure could be helpful for determining how the availability of travel training influences the decision to receive travel training. This new procedure is similar to that of turning the rail line off and on. This procedure will require a switch on the interface titled *close-travel-training-sites*. The command *close-travel-training-sites* should be inserted under the series of *to go* commands.

A second procedure that could be included would be the role of employment programs in influencing people with disabilities to receive travel training. Currently the assumption for this model is that people with disabilities compete with people without disabilities for employment. This model does not include an employment program option for people with disabilities where they do not have to compete with people without disabilities for positions. However, they may receive a lower rate of compensation for their work compared to competitive employment. The employment options could be created in the model by (1) changing some of the competitive employment patches to a different color, and (2) entering a different amount of energy. This can be accomplished by changing several worksite patches from *cyan* to *pink* in the *setup patches* procedure. Insert this revised command from above into the *regrow grass* procedure.

Example 2: Housing Patterns for Persons with Disabilities

In this facsimile model, we demonstrate how different factors, such as gradual integration and having social support within a community, affects participation in the community by a person with disabilities. Following an initial discussion of the model's development, we will explain how traditional research methods were used to create it.

The first component of the model, that it is agent-based, refers to individuals or small groups who become the *evaluands* (the people of interest in the evaluation) in social service organizations. They are the *agents* within a CAS framework. They make decisions from their available and perceived options. With roots in economic game theory, CAS emphasizes the importance of unintended consequences arising from the interactions of heterogeneous agents as they apply simple rules to their behavior. These agents then decide whether it is in their best interest to act alone or to work cooperatively to maximize benefits (Axelrod, 1997; Mankiewicz, 2001). To begin the modeling process, it again becomes useful to fashion it as a complex system using the framework presented in chapter 2.

This model illustrates the desegregation and integration of people with disabilities from institutional care into community-based care. It demonstrates integration through spatial dispersal of agents from one centralized location in the model. To make the spatial model more relevant to temporal changes, two time frames are added. First it's assumed that at the initial point in time, all of the agents (persons with disabilities) lived in the same institution. The second time frame reflects the movement toward social inclusion that took hold in the 1970s, when these people were encouraged through various social support services to live more independently (e.g., in group homes).

This model includes 240 agents. Eighty agents were asked to set their default position at (0,0) and set their color to red, while the remaining agents were asked to randomly select their starting point. All the agents are told to form groups in the mode based on the group size; however, the agents starting at the center have been given directions to limit their movements based on the iterations in the model. So red agents will move forward one space for the first five iterations, stop moving for iterations six through nine, and then continue moving for iterations ten through fifteen. The agents will continue to move for five iterations, then stop for the next five iterations, over the first thirty iterations. After thirty iterations, the 80 red agents will be fully integrated into the groups formed by the other agents.

To track the integration of the red agents in the model, three separate patch colors are used: white, grey, and black. As red agents begin to move from the center of the model to outer edges, they change the color of the patches from white and grey to black. The change in patch color is plotted on the graph in the interface. As the agents level of integration increases the number of black patches increases and the number of grey and white patches decreases. This sample code is in Appendix B. This model is again relatively simple and can be further developed to incorporate the variables that represent community inclusion. Additions to the model could include a procedure that required people without disabilities to report to the observer the number of people with disabilities that they are grouped with at the conclusion of the model. This procedure could include the people without disabilities changing the color of the patches around them and the model graphing the number the patches that had their color change. This procedure requires using the paint-in-radius command for agents representing people without disabilities to identify and graph communities they join. An example of this procedure is outlined below. Insert this command into the pre-existing plot and update the plot on the interface:

set-current-plot-pen "blue patches"
plot count patches with [pcolor = blue]

Another procedure that may be able to improve on this model would be looking for how people with disabilities in the model respond to segregation and inclusion when they have ties with family, friends, and allies without disabilities who are living in the community. This could be simulated with the *create-link-to* and *free-tie* commands, examples of which are provided in the next modified example.

For this procedure, the observer must decide the number of people with disabilities that should have connections in the community, the number of connections each person should have, and identify which agents (people with disabilities) should have those connections.

Modified Example 2 and Traditional Research Methods

The previous models have provided a framework on creating an agent-based model using NetLogo. The models were relatively simple and explored one or two variables. The following revision to Example 2 includes multiple variables in an attempt to incorporate the findings of a study that used spatial autocorrelation and regression analysis in evaluating the community inclusion of people with disability. This demonstrates how a fully developed model appears and the appropriate writing format for presenting an ABM model (Appendix C).

The model assumes three different groups of people: people without disabilities (designated with the color green), people with disabilities living near or with people without disabilities (designated by the color white), people with disabilities and not living near or with people without disabilities (designated by the color red). As the simulation runs, all people expend energy through movement. If their energy reaches zero, then they are no longer able to participate and are removed from the program. Ability to participate is measured by the population of groups remaining in the program. All people can regain energy through eating and using the transit system.

The procedures for the model included 101 people and directing the majority of them to set their color to green, but asking a random number of 16 people to set their color to white or red. People are then assigned into groups based on their color. Those with the color red are segregated from the rest of the population, while people with the color white are placed in groups with green people. The *setup-energy* procedure allows the user to control the initial energy of all people. The *green-setup-energy* slide button controls energy for people without disabilities (color = green) or the *mobility* slide button for people with disabilities (colors = red or white). The user also controls the amount of energy/support that people with color white receive from green people with the *living-in-community* slide button.

The *to go* procedures tells the people to move from one house to the next, how far they can move in a iteration, how much energy to use, and how to use the rail line. It also tells the model to count iterations. The *turn-rail-line-on-off* procedure tells the model which patches to use as the transit system and when to turn them on or off. There is a switch on the interface that will turn the rail line on or off. The procedures *to eat* and *check-death* tell the people to get energy by changing the color of their patches from yellow to black and exiting the model when their energy is equal to zero. *Regrow-grass* and *do-plots* tell the model to change the color of the patches back to yellow and instructs the model to graph the population of the different groups of people in the model.

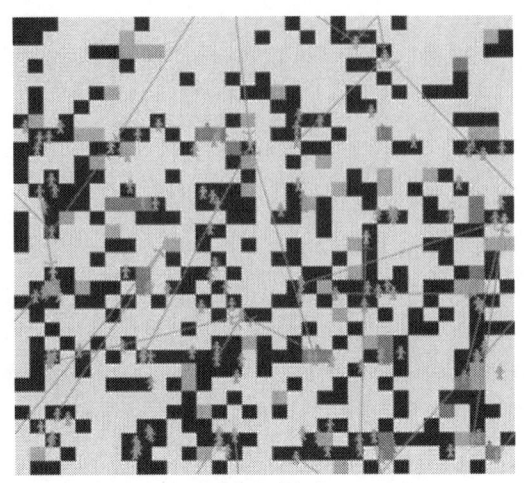

Figure 7.1 Example of the Agent-Based Model when Running.

INTERPRETING AGENT-BASED MODEL RESULTS

NetLogo generates two images when running a program: the model while it is running (Figure 7.1) and a plot tracking the effects of the agent's behavior on the various dependent variables being studied (Figure 7.2).

ABM results can be used as predictive tools for future interventions or policy decisions. But before using ABM as a predictive tool, it should first be used as a compliment to existing research. This will not only aid the observer in validating the model, but it will also give the observer a foundation and framework in which to work to develop ABM as a predictive tool.

ABM results should be interpreted by identifying patterns that emerge over the course of conducting multiple simulations. During ABM simulation, the observer should manipulate the different independent variables, recording the results—not the visual results reported on the interface viewer, but the results reported on the plot.

WRITING AND DISSEMINATING AGENT-BASED MODELS

As proposed by Gilbert (2008), ABMs disseminated in academic literature may require slight modifications from what we have become accustomed.

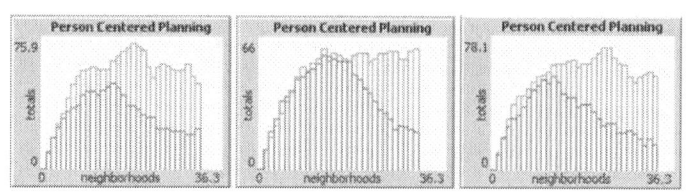

Figure 7.2 Example of Output Generated in NetLogo.

The following outline highlights the salient aspects. (An example of an agent-based modeling report is in Appendix C)

1. The abstract should include the main research question being considered, the findings, the conclusions of the paper, and the methods used.
2. The introduction sets out the background of the issue addressed in the paper and explains why it is of interest.
3. The literature review should discuss previous work and shows why the research reported in this paper is a worthwhile addition or improvement on the prior work. This section should review all relevant information and previous work, and discuss why this is work is an advance.
4. The statement of regularities should include a review of the information provided thus far, followed by the hypothesis that you aim to disprove or prove.
5. The description of the model needs to be sufficiently detailed so that the model can be replicated with the same results, but the description should not include the program code. Particular attention should be paid to the sequence of events that occur in the model to assist with replicating it.
6. In the description of the parameters, the values you have chosen for each parameter should be explained and justified, whether they were from social observations or educated guesses.
7. The description of the results will involve presenting graphs and commenting on the trends illustrated in the graphs. Be sure to provide enough information in the graphs so the reader can be relatively sure that the trends are sustainable throughout the model.

8. A discussion of what steps were taken to verify and validate the model will convey what confidence the reader should place in your results.
9. The conclusion should refer back to the hypothesis, and discuss whether it is true, false, or not proven. The conclusion can continue to develop ideas proposed in the introduction and possibly speculate on the implications.
10. An acknowledgement would thank sponsors, funders, and those who helped with the research.
11. The list of references contains works cited in the paper and no others.
12. The appendix includes tables and possibly the pseudo-code version of model.

SUMMARY

Those seeking a greater understanding on modeling are encouraged to read Epstein (2006) for detailed accounts of studies in agent-based computational modeling in the social sciences.[2] As the concluding chapter explains, complexity in social work can be approached from multiple angles. Being sure to frame the line of inquiry as a complex system remains paramount to developing an understanding of the approach.

EXERCISE

Becoming oriented to the NetLogo software takes a bit of practice. As an initial step, take a model from the NetLogo library and modify it so that it models some social work issue or concern of yours.

8

Concluding Remarks and Proposed Research Agenda

I have experienced a vast range of opportunities as a social work educator and administrator. These opportunities included the provision of services to, and inquiry into improving the quality of life for, persons with intellectual and developmental disabilities, people who abuse substances, people with mental health issues, those who have been trafficked, and immigrant children. Throughout these experiences many commonalities appeared. My overarching purpose for this book has been to introduce complexity theory to social workers and to use this as an organizing framework to generalize my experiences. In much the same manner that the foundational year of a master of social work education focuses on generalist practice, complexity theory provides a generalizable approach for social work researchers and educators.

These concluding remarks and the proposed research agenda will provide the reader with suggestions on the trajectory of complexity and related agent-based models within social work research and evaluation (Figure 8.1). The concepts of complex systems introduced in chapter 1 form the basis for a research agenda for readers to consider in three

1. Theoretical and Conceptual Issues
   a. Approaches using social entrepreneurship
   b. Role of neuroscience
   c. Application of fractals
   d. Identification of power laws within social work
   e. Delineation of how agents involved in social services self-organize
   f. Study of systemic risk
2. Methodological Issues
   a. Developmental evaluation to facilitate innovative learning networks
   b. Social innovation as a vehicle for social change
   c. Cultivation and evaluation of networks designed to facilitate community improvement
   d. Application of egocentric social network analysis to eco-maps
   e. Continued improvement of spatial methods and mapping
   f. Simplified computational methods for use by social service organizations
   g. Creation of mutually reinforcing learning networks with diverse participants
3. Social Work Education and Practice
   a. Encouragement of complexity as a complementary theory
   b. Application of robustness to create resilient ecosystems
   c. Discussion of non-linear methods in research coursework

Figure 8.1 A Social Work Research and Evaluation Agenda.

areas: theoretical/conceptual, methodological, and social work education. This agenda has great importance as organizations ranging from the National Institutes of Health and the Society for Social Work and Research acknowledge the growing importance of systems research.

The learning objectives for this final chapter are

- reviewing the range of applications that complex systems will have in the development of social work education and research methods;

- determining how using complexity fits into your research agenda.

Never doubt that a small group of committed citizens can change the world. Indeed, it is the only thing that ever has

—Margaret Mead, 1928

COMPLEXITY THEORY AS AN ORGANIZING FRAMEWORK

This final chapter discusses social work related issues and conceptualizes a social work oriented research agenda based on complexity theory. As demonstrated, complexity has broad applications to social work research and program evaluation. The intent of this chapter is to provide an initial agenda based on my experiences. Among the advantages of such an approach is that complexity builds upon Patton's utilization-focused evaluation (2008) by fostering use by the intended users of research and evaluation, being active-reactive-interactive-adaptive, and facilitating developmental evaluation that focus on program outcomes and development. To review, the purposes addressed in this book so far include

- providing an alternative research paradigm for social workers to consider and use;
- introducing this paradigm by explaining the concepts behind it and the components that comprise complex systems;
- providing research and program evaluation contexts in which this paradigm is applicable for social work inquiry;
- introducing agent-based modeling (ABM) as one method for understanding complex systems.

This final chapter completes these objectives by suggesting research directions to pursue for social workers interested in complexity theory.

Complexity oriented models best perform when empowered agents select services from program options based on the information they receive. This suggests that the social program planners and staff do not simply follow the status quo when designing services, but rather encourage innovation and cooperation to address their clients' continually changing availability to reliable information, so these clients may make more informed decisions that better address their strengths, needs, abilities, and preferences.

When reviewing this book's purpose—providing an organizing framework for researchers and evaluators—we find that challenges exist when applying complex adaptive systems to measure the collective behavior of agents, rather than simply measuring the aggregated outcomes of programs. These challenges must be addressed by defining the boundaries of models, verifying the reliability and validity of the models, keeping the models agent-based, and deciding when a CAS approach best fits (Epstein, 2006).

New media tools such as social networks, Skype, and blogs provide promising platforms for evaluation communities to self-organize, share information, problem solve, and facilitate multidisciplinary collaboration (Hollingshead & Contractor, 2006). These tools facilitate new opportunities for networking and potentially shared decision making. These evolving researcher and consumer networks will more readily maximize the benefits of collaborations resulting from the skills and perceptions of people with diverse abilities. We recognize the value of the wisdom of crowds.

Available statistical and mathematical tools (e.g., social network analysis, game theory) can converge with new media tools to provide a cohesive toolbox. As complexity theory and the related tools to implement it into program evaluation and research evolve, Miller and Page (2007) remind us of the mindfulness of blending theory and rigorous methodologies. They apply the Buddhist *Eightfold Path* of right view, right intention, right speech, right action, right livelihood, right effort, right mindfulness, and right concentration to suggest a useful mindset when applying complexity to research and evaluation efforts.

A COMPLEXITY ORIENTED SOCIAL WORK AGENDA

Complexity theory can be applied to several aspects of social work research and evaluation. With the increasingly rigorous expectations for social program personnel to be responsive to funding, licensing, and accreditation requirements, a complex systems methodology provides a framework for grounding program assessment activities. Complex systems models work best with longitudinal and spatial data while being applicable to nonexperimental data sets. Because the approach uses an iterative process and a priori information contained in the programs' management information systems, it generates multidimensional perspectives of social work phenomena.

Based on my initial experiences into complexity and social work research and evaluation, three research agenda areas appear ready for development: theoretical/conceptual, methods, and social work education. Within each, the related concepts of chaos and equilibrium, conflict and cooperation, diverse perspectives and diverse heuristics to solve difficult social problems, robustness and resiliency, and self-similarity and scalability are present.

Several agenda items on the application of complexity will be discussed briefly. From a conceptual perspective, issues centering on self-similarity, power laws, and scalability should be addressed. From a methodological perspective, at a minimum, promising lines of inquiry include self-organizing and/or emergent behavior studies, inquiry into the robustness or resiliency of social systems, and game theory applications. Practice issues span from clinical practice to community practice. Relevant topics include applying findings from neuroscience, developing simple-to-use templates for social program evaluators working with organizations and, from a macro perspective, using complexity to apply recent federal legislation concerning creating livable communities. Based on reading a broad base of sources on complexity, and having familiarity with social work education, I suggest the following agenda for furthering a line of study oriented around complexity theory.

Theoretical/Conceptual Issues

Use of complexity in social work can evolve in a manner similar to how the Santa Fe Institute (SFI) developed. SFI has broad interdisciplinary research areas including behavioral dynamics, evolution and emergence, information and computation, physics, and robustness and innovation. This sweeping approach appears readily adoptable by social workers given our interest in social justice, income distribution, psychological methods, social justice, and educational issues. We are the discipline that applies the social sciences to alleviate injustices and improve quality of life across diverse populations.

An example of this new line of inquiry is behavioral economics, where the assumption is made that agents are not necessarily rational, but instead may operate with unconscious motives. This field applies cognitive neuroscience in order to inquire how the unconscious mind uses many vague variables. This is opposed to the conscious mind that uses fewer, but more clearly defined, variables to reach decisions (Dijksterhuis & Nordgren, 2006).

Recently several colleagues and I were discussing how to make our department more relevant and, for lack of a better term, hipper. We were tossing around several ideas, but what struck me was that we were really thinking of including students in some form of social innovation. Social services is primarily geared toward not-for-profit organizations that provide a series of interventions designed to address one or more needs of individuals seeking assistance. These organizations receive funding from governmental sources, foundations, and donations. Despite recent abuses by for-profit lenders to marginalized lendees in micro finance programs (Karnani, 2011), other approaches of social entrepreneurship continue to play an expanding role in social service delivery in market-based economies.[1] Tight federal budgets will continue, and providers of social services need to seek and obtain additional private funding and resources to sustain current provision levels. An example of such social entrepreneurialism that most readers will recognize is the brand Newman's Own, which uses all of its profits to support the hole in the wall camps and progressive political causes.

The role of neuroscience plays an increasingly noticeable role (Farmer, 2009), although the benefits it presents—gaining insight into human behavior—are still overlooked in the direct practice of social work. Neuroscience will be particularly important as the capacity for evidence-based practice evolves (Matto & Strolin-Goltzman, 2010).

On a more abstract level, the Mandelbrot Set refers to a set of fractals that includes items having a shape that contains an infinite amount of fine detail. Presently I cannot say how fractal geometry applies to social work, but some enterprising doctoral student may pick up on this as a research topic. Enhancing this potentially useful approach can occur through applying the concept of fractals and power laws (Clauset, Shalizi, & Newman, 2007; Prigogine, 1996) across theory and practice settings. Specifically this includes the writing of goals and objectives, determining need at different levels, and planning interventions whether at the individual or community level.

Although usually not recognized, complexity displays itself at several levels within social work. We all experience this, as people with diverse backgrounds share common interests and concerns. Self-organizing behavior occurs when a small group of citizens attempt to address what they view as a need in their community. As seen in mutual support groups, such as Alcoholics Anonymous, any individual with a specific need looks for support from others with similar needs. These and countless other social service examples have commonalities in addressing their concerns through complex adaptive systems that are both responsive to the immediate need and flexible enough to adapt as fiscal and program situations evolve.

Systemic risk explores the downside of a highly interconnected and dependent environment. Observers of the financial market collapse of 2008 can attest to the problem of groupthink, whereby a set of deeply cohesive individuals seek to reduce conflict or obtain consensus in a group without the benefit of analyzing their environment critically (McCauley, 1989). Because individuals and their networks are interconnected, these highly linked systems may also serve as contagions. Complexity theory addresses this potential problem through using diverse perspectives and heuristics for problem solving and, therefore, assuring a greater likelihood of creating robustness. The role of diverse heuristics gains acceptance as the quest for solving complicated social problems becomes increasingly interdisciplinary (Norman, Best, Mortimer, Huerta, & Buchan, 2011). The role of contagion is easily seen in epidemics and more recently in the role of programmed trading in the financial markets (Goldin, 2010).

Methodological Issues

While complex systems have become an accepted natural and social paradigm, social work researchers and evaluators have barely begun to apply it. The social work literature has begun a dialogue on complexity; however, the development of a functional model has received limited attention. Developmental evaluation and facilitating innovative learning networks may become one line for future inquiry as these methods seek to use the impact of research as a quantitative measure (Saari & Kallio, 2011).

A promising literature has emerged addressing the related concept of social innovation that introduces interconnected components of complexity and efforts to create social change. This broad concept of social innovation—often involving individuals from disciplines including business, social development, and economics—most often occurs outside the social work discipline. This appears to be an unfortunate turn of events as social work students increasingly seek degrees in clinical practice at the expense of the macro-oriented practice of social change.

As one undergirding framework, Malinsky and Lubesky (2011), from the Centre for Social Innovation in Toronto, propose an approach for cultivating and evaluating networks designed to facilitate community improvement, and it centers on three core concepts: social change, complexity theory, and listening to networks. Materials from their ready-to-use toolkit provide an introduction for social service practitioners in applying complex systems thought. These studies can occur through applied studies or conceptually. Applied studies may focus on computational (also known as simulation or generative studies) issues or game theory—in which the choices agents make are based on various influences (Deng & Chu, 2011).

Computational or generative studies using agent-based modeling, network analysis, neural networks, and spatial geographic methods suit program planning and community practice particularly well. ABM may for a brief period play the role of an intellectual exercise within the social service realm until the programming of such models becomes simplified. This may follow a similar path that occurred in the adoption and use of geographic information systems (GIS) in social work.

Systems dynamics modeling (and related simulations) suggest another methodology for consideration because it expresses temporal cause-and-effect relationships between variables. This methodology uses mathematical modeling to frame, understand, and share complex issues. It does not, however, represent agents directly and therefore is not a true bottom-up approach (Gilbert, 2008). Since being developed in the middle of the twentieth century to assist managers improve their understanding of processes, system dynamics has since been applied throughout the public and private sector for policy analysis and design. System dynamics recognizes that the structure of any system contains circular, interlocking, and often time-lagged relationships within its components. Users of systems dynamics believe in the importance of understanding the entire system more than the behavior of the individual components (Senge, 2006; Sterman, 2000).

As the divide between qualitative and quantitative researchers diminishes, methods, including concept mapping (Kane & Trochim, 2007), appear ready to integrate into an evaluator or researcher's toolbox when using the complexity paradigm. Paramount to social work is using complexity to blend the benefits of qualitative and quantitative research methods. Qualitative research applies inductive reasoning to social work processes, and uses nonnumerical data to answer exploratory inquiries. Conversely, quantitative research relies on a deductive approach and applies numerical data to measure outcomes through hypothesis testing.

Future development applications include defining a concise set of prompts for defining the components, outlining appropriate statistical procedures to analyze the data, and creating viable procedures and templates for program planners and evaluators. This approach provides the benefits of looking at whole systems and their interconnections and modeling micro interactions among persons/agents, and then chaining the two models together to identify how changes in access affect the search for services of individuals, families, and units of measure.

Infusing complexity into everyday assessment, planning, and practice will be supported by conducting additional research on developing reliability and validity studies on instruments that measure the strength of egocentric networks. This includes further testing of recently developed instruments (e.g., Alemi, Stephens, Llorens, Schaefer, Nemes, & Arendt, 2003). Such instruments will increasingly provide initial metrics for measuring complexity related concepts, such as the strength and robustness of support networks, and may be applied to specific social work populations.

Given the increasing availability of evaluation tools and computing power, complexity provides a promising and salient framework. It has a widening appeal for analyzing quantitative (numerical) and qualitative (nonnumerical) data. We envision this when attempting to improve a person's ability to recognize patterns through spatial autocorrelation and other iterative models. Additional efforts should focus on making instruments that measure emergent trends over time and space more accessible to organizational planners, administrators, and others.

Recent efforts to simulate social networks suggest another branch for inquiry (Hamill & Gilbert, 2010). Understanding how agent-based modeling applies directly to social work research will soon become apparent. As our field continues to align with experimental, quasi-experimental, and various qualitative methods, we need to remain cognizant that social change is dynamic. Conducting research on the dynamic tendencies of social change justifies further theoretical inquiry into simulation and the application of ABM.

One possible area is force field analysis (FFA). Developed by Kurt Lewin (1943), this technique creates a process for problem solving and managing change. It is based on two assumptions: in every situation there are forces driving change and forces resisting change, and an emphasis on reducing resisting forces is more efficient than increasing driving forces. When conducting an FFA, the evaluator identifies and lists the forces impinging on a situation. This typically follows a five-step process that includes describing the change issue and the desired direction of change; listing the political forces driving that change and those restraining it, and illustrating the forces of opposition in a diagram; giving a weight to the forces, realizing that some are stronger and more powerful than others; focusing on the restraining forces, and assessing which significant ones need and those that can be worked on; and developing a plan for reducing the forces (Coghlan & Brannick, 2005).

Limitations that require additional consideration include small sample sizes and instances where there has been a restructuring of data, typically those collected by human service organizations. In the first situation, organizational decision makers may have access to data on a limited number of individuals and need to make and justify decisions using these small samples. Because of these small samples, current analyses may provide limited information; robust methods are needed to improve the information these decision makers must use. In the second situation, data collected by organizations may require restructuring to implement more powerful measures and statistical approaches for their current organizational data sets.

Social service organizations benefit by a mixed-model approach, where both qualitatively based process information and quantitatively based outcome measures are used in decision making. Administrators of these organizations need to avail themselves to a range of data sources that include both qualitative (nonnumeric) and quantitative (numeric) data.

Outcome monitoring and quality improvement methods remain vital to improving the efficacy of human services organizations. Current organizational evaluative and improvement methods concentrating only on output of services (e.g., cost per unit of services, number of clients provided services in a given time period) cannot account for the constantly changing environment in which these organizations operate. Basic evaluation research, therefore, on methods to determine and apply benchmarks within a complexity theory, grows in importance.

Turning to program evaluation, because ABM allows us the means to visualize emergent group behavior based on individual characteristics, it is ripe for use by organizations needing an efficient tool. One area of development is to create simplified methods for those with limited computational skills to be able to use. These easy-to-use techniques become increasingly important, as resources shrink in human service organizations that provide direct practice with individuals and their families. Given the increasing availability of evaluation tools and computing power, complexity provides a promising framework for creating *in silico* platforms for practice, education, and research.

Complexity has a growing potential for blending and analyzing quantitative and qualitative data. Integrating a complexity perspective with standard program evaluation techniques, such as logic modeling, GANTT charts, flow charts, and PERT charts, needs further development in order for complex systems to firmly become applicable within social service organizations. Williams and Hummelbrunner (2011) proposed a toolkit for using complexity and the more generalized systems concepts in program evaluation that builds upon this base by first understanding the dynamic tendencies found in social service delivery systems. The evaluator's ability to recognize patterns increases as spatial autocorrelation and other iterative models that measure emergent trends over time and space become more accessible.

Assuming that social programs respond continually to funding and accreditation requirements, a CAS framework provides a broad conceptual approach for program evaluators. Complex system models work best with the longitudinal and spatial data sets present in social service organizations that have or that are seeking accreditation. Because complexity encourages the use of an iterative process and a priori information contained in management information systems, it generates multidimensional perspectives of social service phenomena.

At the end of chapter 2, a rudimentary exercise was presented to assist in framing inquiry into the complexity framework that was provided.

Future efforts to develop applications in social program evaluation may include delineating a concise set of prompts for defining the components, and creating viable procedures and checklists for program planners and evaluators to use.

Social Work Education and Practice

Social workers facilitate change in order to address the issues of human rights, poverty, and the environment. Complexity theory provides a promising approach for understanding and evaluating outcomes (Wolf-Branigin, 2009). Applying complexity means we are developing our knowledge, skills, and ability to understand the interconnectedness and exigencies present within our clients' systems. This occurs through developing mutually reinforcing learning groups with people from diverse backgrounds and viewpoints.

As I have stressed throughout, social work researchers and educators considering complexity in their coursework or research methods should recognize that successful application relies on exploratory methods through pattern recognition rather than traditional experimental hypothesis testing. Social work managers and planners often function in a quantitative world, whereas practitioners are in a qualitative world.

Beyond the theoretical and methodological issues of complexity, areas in which social work educators may become involved include the generalist concepts, which are consistent with self-similarity. These include

- discussing application from a social policy perspective (federal, state, local, community /agency);
- writing goals and objectives (in the same method used for social program evaluation or client records);
- conducting need assessment at client, organizational, and community levels;
- determining how scale-free (fractal) applications apply to social work education (fractals, the presence of repeated patterns and multiple levels or scales, can apply to issues such as assessing need, developing goals and objectives, and policy analysis).

As a start, we should encourage that social work research texts begin addressing complex systems as a complementary approach for investigating social work phenomena. This paradigm needs to become an accepted viewpoint in our discipline as we apply evidence-based practice and translational research into our research programs.

Whether at the macro level (Tenkasi & Chesmore, 2003) or micro level (Hudson, 2004), creating robust social support systems will encourage individuals, families, and communities to be resilient to ecosystem threats (Watts & Strogatz, 1998). Generalist social work educators, focusing on teaching essential skills that can be applied to a variety of situations, can supplement their complexity related skills. In generalist social work, the same tools are needed for understanding and assessing environments; creating robust organizations, families, or individuals; improving evaluation at both the client and program level; and planning at the client and program level.

Self-similarity as a social work education issue exists whether it involves working in partnership with the person served in developing their goals and objectives, or creating goals and objectives for a social program evaluation. This reinforcing of such generalist social work skills can be strengthened and become a conceptual research focus.

Applications cut across different system levels as the concept of robustness–resilience have well-documented implications for clinical work with individuals and families. These have additional implications for macro practice when we consider the need to create robust organizations by eliminating threats to organizational sustainability. For example, building in staffing redundancies and cross-training of staff makes the organization less vulnerable when one or two key staff people leave for other opportunities. Coursework dealing with social program evaluation and the application of these methods likewise suits complexity well.

The National Association of Social Workers' Code of Ethics states that our mission rests on a set of core values, including service, social justice, the dignity and worth of the person, importance of human relationships, integrity, and competence (National Association of Social Workers, 2007). Complex systems theory and successful social work practice share several assumptions. These include: (1) that decisions should come from the client level or grassroots level, (2) that attractors are instrumental in clients maintaining interest and completing interventions, (3) that successful outcomes result frequently from the interactions of latent combinations of variables, and (4) that client and organizational feedback are vital to improving outcomes and organizational performance.

As the American educational system increasingly focuses on science, technology, engineering, and mathematics (STEM) curriculum, the adoption of complexity within social work curricula suggests a natural home for increasing the quantitative skills for future practitioners. This is seen in the contributions of mathematicians including Godel (principle of computability; (Casti & DePauli, 2000, pp. 81–83), Descartes (coordinate system), Mandelbrot (fractals), Euler (graph theory), & Nash (game theory). Although we may prefer to solve simple problems, another area of study involves the issue of wicked questions (Zimmerman, 2000). These problems cannot be answered with traditional analytic methods, because such questions typically involve a high level of uncertainty.

Given that community need is elastic in that it changes over time, complexity theory, when used with agent-based modeling, provides a salient tool for simulating and visually forecasting needs into the future. Because of its use of individual, bottom-up information, the resulting emergent behavior contributes to government and organizational planners being able to address needs. Economic development from the asset acquisition perspective remains a line of inquiry eager for further development. Whether at the personal, family, or organization level, having the sufficient capital or cash on hand improves the viability of these units. Further work applying human capital theory and asset building (Schreiner & Sherraden, 2007; Sherraden & Barr, 2005) needs to occur.

Geographic information systems and mapping methods support the application of complexity theory in social work education by aiding in understanding the influences of location on human behavior, identifying community needs and assets, and providing community members who have traditionally been disenfranchised from decision making (Hillier, 2007). Geographic approaches, such as layering characteristics to assist in visualizing the influences of additional variables on an issue, needs further refinement.

When developing robust systems, social workers can focus on social network analysis (SNA), where measures such as density and prestige are used. SNA typically includes egocentric models to investigate the strength of individual networks that potentially can lead to developing highly quantifiable eco-maps and genograms. A related future line of inquiry may focus on applications available for mobile devises. For example, recent apps such as *Klout* for *Twitter* can measure the prestige a user has within a social network.

FINAL COMMENTS

Taleb (2010) notes that globalization creates an interconnected fragility. This fragility arises in the social services sector as program designs and interventions become generalized across populations without sufficient evidence of their success. The continual interaction of parts is needed for complex systems to operate effectively. A pile of junk may have diverse parts, but these parts do not interact; it's just a pile of junk (Page, 2011). To successfully integrate complexity theory into your research and evaluation toolbox, users must grasp the continual interaction of agents and how these agents use of feedback to reach an emergent behavior. In this sense, complexity is a long process of combining and winnowing.

Complexity theory should not be viewed simply as an alternative to empirical evidence-based practice, but rather as a complement to it, by understanding better the environments and exigencies that exist. Taleb (2010) further notes that human thought and cognition has not evolved as rapidly as the complicated environments in which we all live. Therefore, our decision-making abilities lead us to overvalue recent events when anticipating the future, and then to construct a single, disproportionate perspective to problem solving. This process often relies on recent personal outcomes that were positive but that likely occurred because of lucky events rather than the benefit of individual and collective action. Introducing complex systems into coursework also may aid students in learning how to deal with the ambiguity they will all too often have to address in macro and micro practice.

During the past decade, a debate has emerged regarding how social work delivery systems will address the digital divide, as represented by access to the Internet and the broader digital environment. This issue includes both the recipients' and the providers' perspectives. Clients need access to technology to assure equitable and effective receipt of services (Steyaert & Gould, 2009), while providers fear displacement from face-to-face social service encounters will lead to ones that are more accountable and bureaucratic information-based (Burton & van den Broek, 2008). Further discussion regarding the divide focuses on the lack of access to the Internet and other digital technology needed.

As the digital divide appears to decrease and Internet access for social workers and their clientele continually improves, a new specialty of social work informatics may evolve (Parker-Oliver & Demiris, 2006). The computational aspects of such an emerging specialty will dovetail with complexity theory, as layers of data may assist in identifying patterns of behaviors and decisions that previously had appeared random. The computational aspects of complexity theory will play an increasing role in synthesizing this vast trough of information. New technologies increasingly provide access for innovators to link their programming efforts and access input from a variety of stakeholders (Scearce, Kasper, & McLeod, 2010). These efforts are becoming more open, transparent, and decentralized. Therefore, one research area in theoretical applications will be on developing decision support systems that result from the increasing presence of evidence-based practices with specific populations. This should be accomplished through data systems that the persons served by social work organizations and their workers assess and use.

About six years ago, the application of social innovation piqued my interest in making complex systems the framework for my research agenda. I found this interesting because it reminded me that one of the earliest schools of social work—the University of Chicago—initially known as the Chicago School of Civics and Philanthropy—evolved from involvement in the Settlement House Movement and encouraged linking those with many resources to support people with limited options. The question arises, will social service personnel, as Light (2011) states, just maintain and be safe keepers of social innovations, or will we be facilitators of it?

Social innovators apply complexity theory in creating their interventions to alleviate social problems (Libert & Spector, 2008). Creating the innovative linkages between social concepts that inform program planners and evaluators can be challenging. Light (2011) notes four different forms of social drivers when seeking change through social innovation. In the first, if a new breakthrough involves a combination of ideas, then social entrepreneurship—in the form of investment from outside sources—will be the primary driver for change. Secondly, if the breakthrough requires that the protection, repair, or maintain, then an approach requiring social safeguarding will be the best approach. Third, if the breakthrough focuses on anticipating threats, monitoring emerging trends, or evaluating what works, then social exploring likely will provide the preferred approach. Finally, breakthroughs addressing policy impacts require an advocacy approach that includes lobbying and pressure tactics. Social innovation projects, because of their unique approaches, need to obtain public and financial support. Marketing such efforts may require creative online avenues that assure powerful, focused, and well-defined electronic social networking (Aaker & Smith, 2010; Leroux Miller, 2010).

As the arena of social innovation gains momentum, will we expect to see what Fogel (2000) described as the Fourth Great Awakening? When assuming that government resources for supporting social initiatives will become increasingly limited, will the faith-based community play a greater role in delivering initiatives that support social justice? The jury remains out. As social innovative programs expand in business and other areas to support social issues, they are not without controversy. Well-recognized and regarded organizations including the Grameen Bank and Kiva have become vulnerable. Grameen faces controversy because of possible lending abuses (Karnani. 2011) while Kiva has been subjected to false marketing claims (Aaker & Smith, 2010).

In juxtaposition to the chaos exhibited by the butterfly effect, Aaker and Smith (2010) propose the metaphor of a dragonfly effect to facilitating social change through the coordination of the four wings required for the dragonfly to move. Their book, *The Dragonfly Effect*, concentrates on using social media in the form of creating robust networks for cultivating social change. They advocate a four aspect (wings) approach by (1) focusing on how to hatch a goal that will make an impact, (2) grabbing attention in an overcrowded, over-messaged world, (3) engaging with others on how to connect people to your goal, and (4) taking action to empower and enable others to cultivate a movement. Leroux Miller (2010) similarly advances the use of social media, but more for the marketing of existing programs and services.

In their book, *Getting to Maybe: How the World Is Changed*, Westley, Zimmerman, and Patton (2006) proposed a model for achieving social change by drawing together three interdependent concepts—social innovation, complexity science, and developmental evaluation. From their viewpoint, applying complexity theory involves two principal assumptions, (1) the holistic concept that the system's parts cannot explain the whole, and (2) that relationships are essential when introducing social innovations. A third assumption involves using an emergence approach rather than what we would typically consider as planning. This emergence approach involves interaction rules that provide clients and decision makers with the necessary tools for working in partnership. These interaction rules lead to emergence and aid in sustaining the innovation.

Developmental evaluation makes organizational learning the primary objective rather than accountability. Within developmental evaluation, Westley, Zimmerman, and Patton suggest using intuition based on strategic and integrated thinking. They conceptualize developmental evaluation as the next wave of evaluation that furthers the sustainability of systems and builds upon both process and outcome evaluation. Successful social innovators know the value of understanding the simple, the complicated, and the complex. The simple represents easy to follow instructions; the complicated states that while a system or phenomena may have apparently countless steps, if followed properly, we can anticipate similar outcomes; but the complex will frequently produce different outcomes when replicated. The evolving idea of developmental evaluation, particularly as it relates to social innovation, suggests an area prime for inquiry by social work researchers and evaluators.

SUMMARY

This final chapter suggests a guide for social work graduate students, researchers, and evaluators to follow as our discipline applies the emerging scientific paradigm of complexity. This provides one lens on what complexity theory and complex systems involve. Consistent with the assumptions of complexity theory, successful implementation and development within our discipline should follow a few of the key components of being agent-based, self-organizing, and creating an emergent behavior. Therefore, for successful implementation to occur, we, as the leaders of this movement, must assure that decisions are not top–down, but rather that they arise from the level of the consumers of the services, students, or faculty interested in creating the necessary partnerships for developing this line of inquiry.

As explained throughout, complexity arises from the interactions of the agents' competitive and cooperative tendencies comprising systems. Such systems are in a continual state of dynamic equilibrium, where they navigate between being in rigid order and chaos. These systems operate according to a set of simple rules, yet patterns emerge from these simple interactions without a predetermined template (Mankiewicz, 2001). Social work shares several attributes found in complex systems theory. These include that decisions come from the grassroots; that attractors maintain an agent's interest in participating and completing interventions; that rules set the boundaries; that feedback is vital to improving outcomes; and that self-organization of these agents creates emergent behavior.

As others across the various academic and professional disciplines have done, a growing social worker cohort worldwide likewise expresses their interest in complexity. Our role is not simply to garner the connections in order to develop our own research agendas, but also to assure that these agendas are interconnected with the social environments in which policies, programs, and services are delivered. A large amount of complex system oriented research occurs in the social sciences, and social work as the discipline that applies this knowledge must integrate this material into practice. As you may notice, when framed in a social work context, we are searching for answers collaboratively with customers of services, rather than planning from top–down.

The remainder of the book provides resources for developing the requisite skills and background for developing your own use of this emerging paradigm. Given the deep theoretical development in the field of complex systems from diverse academic disciplines, this emerging framework appears more than a simple fad. Applying the framework requires a requisite knowledge of the conceptual development. My hope is that a sufficient level of detail was provided, without becoming tiresome.[2]

EXERCISES

1. The area of social innovation has roots in complexity theory. To gain better insight into this, review the websites for the Roosevelt Institute (http://www.rooseveltinstitute.org), Skoll Social Edge (http://www.socialedge.org), the Centre for Social Innovation—Toronto (http://www.socialinnovation.ca), and Stanford University Graduate Business School's Center for Social Innovation (http://www.gsb.stanford.edu/csi/). Suggest how an issue or social work concern you have can be addressed through one of these organizations.
2. Further develop your understanding of the application of complexity theory in social networks by downloading and

reviewing Malinsky and Lubesky's (2011) *Network Evaluation: Cultivating Healthy Networks for Social Change* (http://socialinnovation.ca/networkevaluation). Apply the exercises near the end of the download to a current organizational project on which you may be working.
3. Expand your options of what can be accomplished through complexity by viewing the 53-minute PBS video on Fractals: Hunting the Hidden Dimension (http://www.pbs.org/wgbh/nova/physics/hunting-hidden-dimension.html). Discuss how fractals may apply to a generalist social work education.
4. While the term *social innovation* is relatively new, in practice it has in fact been around a long while. Discuss whether the employee assistance programs developed within various industries were early versions of social innovations. Why or why not?
5. As persons concerned with social change become involved in initiatives to create a social innovation, new tools emerge to support their efforts. One useful model is the *Human Centered Design Toolkit* created by the innovative design firm IDEO (http://www.ideo.com/work/human-centered-design-toolkit/). Download this tool and work through an example of your own.

Appendix A

Coding for Example 1: Travel Training for Persons with Disabilities

```
breed [people person] ;; breed allows for the use of
   different types of agents in a model.
people-own [energy];; people-own sets certain variables as
   belonging to all agents of a ;;certain breed.

to setup
clear-all
setup-patches
create-people 200 ;; creates the number of agents. This
   number can be changed if ;;desired.
ask people [setxy random-xcor random-ycor]
ask people [set color green];;green indicates those without
   a disability
ask n-of 15 people [set color red];;red = has a disability,
   a random group of 15 people ;;will be designated as having
   a disability
ask n-of 15 people [set color black];;black = has a
   disability, a random group of 15 ;;people will be
   designated as having a disability
set-default-shape people "person";; sets the shape of
   moving agents as people instead ;;of the normal default
   shape
```

```
create-rail-line ;; will allow for the creation of a rail
  line later in the procedures
do-plots;; allows for the setup of a plot to monitor energy
do-plots-employment
setup-energy;; allows the observers to later set up a
  procedure to change agents ;;energy.
end

to setup-patches ;; by setting the color of the patches to a
  different color the agents
;; can later change the color back to black as a way to gain
  energy.
ask patches [set pcolor yellow]
;; The following procedures mark patches as being
  employment sites or travel training ;;sites, white
  signifies the travel training sites and cyan represents
  employment ;;opportunities in model.
ask patches with [pxcor > -7 and pxcor < -4 and pycor < 7
  and pycor > 4]
[set pcolor white]
ask patches with [pxcor > 12 and pxcor < 16 and pycor < 2
  and pycor > -2]
[set pcolor white]
ask patches with [pxcor > 5 and pxcor < 9 and pycor < 15 and
  pycor > 10]
[set pcolor white]
ask patches with [pxcor > 3 and pxcor < 9 and pycor < 9 and
  pycor > 3]
[set pcolor Cyan]
ask patches with [pxcor > -9 and pxcor < -3 and pycor > -10
  and pycor < -3]
[set pcolor cyan]
ask patches with [pxcor < 9 and pxcor > 3 and pycor > -10
  and pycor < -3]
[set pcolor cyan]
ask patches with [pxcor > -15 and pxcor < -5 and pycor < 15
  and pycor > 10]
[set pcolor cyan]
ask patches with [pxcor > -2 and pxcor < 5 and pycor > 10
  and pycor < 15]
[set pcolor cyan]
ask patches with [pxcor > -16 and pxcor < -10 and pycor >
  -10 and pycor < 10]
[set pcolor cyan]
ask patches with [pxcor > -9 and pxcor < 9 and pycor > -16
  and pycor < -11]
```

```
[set pcolor cyan]
ask patches with [pxcor > 10 and pxcor < 15 and pycor > 4
    and pycor < 18]
[set pcolor cyan]
ask patches with [pxcor > 10 and pxcor < 15 and pycor < -4
    and pycor > -16]
[set pcolor cyan]
end

to setup-energy;; This procedure sets the setup energy
    for all agents. This allows the ;;observer to change the
    energy of the different agents.
ask people with [color = green]
[set energy (energy + green-setup-independence)];;gree
    n-setup-energy is a sliding ;;button on the interface so
    the observer can change the energy.
ask people with [color = red]
[set energy (energy + disability-setup-independence)];;
    red-setup-energy is a sliding ;;button on the interface.
ask people with [color = black]
[set energy (energy + disability-setup-independence)]
end
;; These procedures tell the agents how to move in the model
    and how those ;;movements will affect their energy output
    or intake.

to go
tick ;; tells the model to count iterations.
;; These procedures set up the nature of the agents
    disabilities which are limits on their ;;mobility and
    increased energy expenditures for movement.
ask people with [color = green]
[fd 3 set energy (energy - 1)]
ask people with [color = red]
[fd 1 set energy (energy - 3)]
ask people with [color = black]
[fd 1 set energy (energy - 3)]

;; These procedures tell the agents how to use the rail line
    and allow the observer to ;;change the energy intake from
    using the rail system.
ask people with [color = green] [if pcolor = gray]
[fd 30 set energy (energy + energy-on-rail-line)] ;; fd
    30 sets the speed in which the ;;agents can use the rail
    system, if desired the observer can change this number.
]
```

Appendix A   153

```
ask people with [color = black] [if pcolor = gray
[fd 30 set energy (energy + energy-on-rail-line)]
]
ask people with [color = red]
[if pcolor = white
[set color black]
]
ask people [if pcolor = cyan
[set energy (energy + 3)]
]
;;these following commands tell the model when to turn the
  rail line on or off, regrow ;;grass, plot energy and track
  available employment
turn-rail-line-on-off
do-plots
do-plots-employment
eat
regrow-grass
end

to create-rail-line ;; This procedure lays out the transit
  system by changing the colors of ;;patches.
ask patches with [pxcor > 2 and pxcor < 4]
[set pcolor gray]
ask patches with [pxcor < -2 and pxcor > -4]
[set pcolor gray]
ask patches with [pycor < -2 and pycor > -4 ]
[set pcolor gray]
ask patches with [pycor > 2 and pycor < 4]
[set pcolor gray]
ask patches with [pxcor > -10 and pxcor < -8]
[set pcolor gray]
ask patches with [pxcor < 10 and pxcor > 8]
[set pcolor gray]
ask patches with [pycor > -11 and pycor < -9]
[set pcolor gray]
ask patches with [pycor < 10 and pycor > 8]
[set pcolor gray]
end

to turn-rail-line-on-off ;; This procedure allows the
  observer to turn the train line on or off ;;to see how
  using to mass transit
;;can affect people with disabilities living in urban areas.
  For the procedure to work ;;each line must be given the
  order individually to turn on or off.
```

```
ask patches with [pxcor < -2 and pxcor > -4 ]
[ifelse turn-rail-line-on-off?;; turn-rail-line-on-off? is
  a switch button on the interface. If ;;the lines are grey
  they are on, if they are blue they are off.
[set pcolor gray]
[set pcolor blue]
]
ask patches with [pycor > 2 and pycor < 4]
[ifelse turn-rail-line-on-off?
[set pcolor gray]
[set pcolor blue]
]
ask patches with [pxcor > 2 and pxcor < 4]
[ifelse turn-rail-line-on-off?
[set pcolor gray]
[set pcolor blue]
]
ask patches with [pycor < -2 and pycor > -4]
[ifelse turn-rail-line-on-off?
[set pcolor gray]
[set pcolor blue]
]
ask patches with [pxcor > -10 and pxcor < -8]
[ifelse turn-rail-line-on-off?
[set pcolor gray]
[set pcolor blue]
]
ask patches with [pxcor < 10 and pxcor > 8]
[ifelse turn-rail-line-on-off?
[set pcolor gray]
[set pcolor blue]
]
ask patches with [pycor > -11 and pycor < -9]
[ifelse turn-rail-line-on-off?
[set pcolor gray]
[set pcolor blue]
]
ask patches with [pycor < 10 and pycor > 8]
[ifelse turn-rail-line-on-off?
[set pcolor gray]
[set pcolor blue]
]
end
to eat ;;By eating agents receive energy, this command
  being used to symbolize the ;;energy gained through
  employment.
```

Appendix A

```
    ask people [if pcolor = cyan [set pcolor black set energy
      (energy + 10)]]
end

to regrow-grass;; This command allows for the patches that
   had their color change black ;;turn back to cyan so other
   agents can use the patches.
   ask patches with [pcolor = black] [if random 25 < 3 [set
      pcolor cyan]]
end

;; While observing a model can be a way of gathering
   information, using graphs provide ;;data and allow the
   observer to run models at a faster speed than observation
   will allow.
;; This plot measures the number of people with training
   through measuring the ;;populations of the two groups.
to do-plots
set-current-plot "training" ;; "training" will be the name
   of the plot on the interface.
set-current-plot-pen "people without disabilities" ;; this
   will track the population of green ;;agents/people with
   out disabilities using the color green.
plot count people with [color = green]
set-current-plot-pen "people with disabilities";; this
   will track the population of red ;;agents/people with
   disabilities using their color
plot count people with [color = red]
set-current-plot-pen "people with travel";;this will track
   the population of black ;;agents/people with disabilities
   using their color
plot count people with [color = black]
end

to do-plots-employment;; this plot is very similar to the
   one above and tracks the level of ;;available employment.
set-current-plot "work"
set-current-plot-pen "available work"
plot count patches with [pcolor = cyan]
end
```

Appendix B

Coding for Example 2: Housing Patterns for Persons with Disabilities

If interested is seeing the code run, you can copy it from the companion website and then paste it into the NetLogo dialog box. Coding for the revised example 2 follows this one.

```
breed [people person]
people-own [energy my-group]

to setup
clear-all
setup-patches
create-people 240
ask people [set color green]
ask n-of 80 people [set color red]
set-default-shape people "person"
ask people with [color = green] [setxy random-xcor
   random-ycor]
setup-plots
setup-energy
end
```

```
to setup-patches
ask patches with [pxcor > -7 and pxcor < 7 and pycor > -7
  and pycor < 7] [set pcolor white]
ask patches with [pxcor > -12 and pxcor < 12 and pycor <
  -6 and pycor > -12] [set pcolor gray]
ask patches with [pxcor > -12 and pxcor < -6 and pycor >
  -7 and pycor < 12] [set pcolor gray]
ask patches with [pxcor > -7 and pxcor < 12 and pycor < 12
  and pycor > 6] [set pcolor gray]
ask patches with [pxcor > 6 and pxcor < 12 and pycor < 7
  and pycor > -12] [set pcolor gray]
end

to setup-energy
ask people with [color = green]
[set energy (energy + 15)]
ask people with [color = red] [set energy (energy + 10)]
end

to go
tick
ask people with [color = red][if my-group != -1 [face
  get-home]]
ask people with [color = red] [if ticks < 5 [fd 1]]
ask people with [color = red] [if ticks > 10 and ticks <
  15 [fd 1]]
ask people with [color = red] [if ticks > 20 and ticks <
  25 [fd 1]]
ask people with [color = red] [if ticks > 30 [fd 3]]
Ask people with [color = green]
[if my-group != -1 [face get-home]
fd 3
set energy (energy - 1)]
update-plots
eat
end

to-report get-home
let side ceiling (sqrt (max [my-group] of people + 1))
report patch
(round ((world-width / side) * (my-group mod side)
+ min-pxcor + int (world-width / (side * 2))))
(round ((world-height / side) * int (my-group / side)
+ min-pycor + int (world-height / (side * 2))))
end
```

```
to assign-by-size
ask people [set my-group -1]
let unassigned people
let current 0
while [any? unassigned]
[
ask n-of (min(list group-size (count unassigned)))
  unassigned
  [set my-group current]
set current current + 1
set unassigned unassigned with [my-group = -1]
]
end

to eat
ask people with [color = red] [if pcolor = white [set
  pcolor black] set energy (energy + 2)]
ask people with [color = red] [if pcolor = grey [set
  pcolor black] set energy (energy + 2)]
end

to setup-plots
update-spatial-plot
end

to update-plots
update-spatial-plot
end

to update-spatial-plot
set-current-plot "Community integration"
set-current-plot-pen "black patches"
plot count patches with [pcolor = black]
set-current-plot-pen "white patches"
plot count patches with [pcolor = white]
set-current-plot-pen "gray patches"
plot count patches with [pcolor = gray]
end
```

CODING FOR THE REVISED EXAMPLE 2

```
Breed [people person]
people-own [energy my-group]
```

```
to setup
clear-all
setup-patches
create-people 150
ask people [set color green]
ask n-of 12 people [set color red]
ask n-of 2 people [set color cyan]
ask person 54 [set color cyan]
ask person 55 [set color cyan]
ask person 56 [set color cyan]
ask person 57 [set color cyan]
ask person 58 [set color cyan]
ask person 59 [set color cyan]
ask person 60 [set color cyan]
ask person 61 [set color cyan]
ask person 62 [set color cyan]
ask person 63 [set color cyan]
ask n-of 1 people with [color = green] [create-link-to
  person 54 [set tie-mode "free"]]
ask n-of 1 people with [color = green] [create-link-to
  person 55 [set tie-mode "free"]]
ask n-of 2 people with [color = green] [create-link-to
  person 56 [set tie-mode "free"]]
ask n-of 2 people with [color = green] [create-link-to
  person 57 [set tie-mode "free"]]
ask n-of 2 people with [color = green] [create-link-to
  person 58 [set tie-mode "free"]]
ask n-of 2 people with [color = green] [create-link-to
  person 59 [set tie-mode "free"]]
ask n-of 3 people with [color = green] [create-link-to
  person 60 [set tie-mode "free"]]
ask n-of 3 people with [color = green] [create-link-to
  person 61 [set tie-mode "free"]]
ask n-of 3 people with [color = green] [create-link-to
  person 62 [set tie-mode "free"]]
ask n-of 3 people with [color = green] [create-link-to
  person 63 [set tie-mode "free"]]
set-default-shape people "person"
ask people [setxy random-xcor random-ycor]
setup-plots
setup-energy
end

to setup-patches
ask patches [set pcolor yellow]
end
```

```
to setup-energy
ask people with [color = green]
[set energy (energy + 15)]
ask people with [color = red] [set energy (energy + 10)]
ask people with [color = cyan] [set energy (energy + 10)]
end

to go
tick
ask people with [color = red][if my-group != -1 [face
  get-home] fd 1 set energy (energy - 3)]
ask people with [color = cyan][if my-group != -1 [face
  get-home] fd 1 set energy (energy - 3)]
ask people with [color = cyan] [show count people-here
  with [color = green]
if count people-here with [color = green] >= 5
[set energy (energy + 10)]
paint-in-radius
]
ask people with [color = red] [show count people-here with
  [color = green]
if count people-here with [color = green] >= 5
[paint-in-radius]
]
ask people with [color = green] [show count people-here
  with [color = cyan]
if count people-here with [color = cyan] >= 3
[set energy (energy + 5)]]
Ask people with [color = green]
[if my-group != -1 [face get-home]
fd 2
set energy (energy - 1)]
eat
regrow-grass
update-plots
end

to-report get-home
let side ceiling (sqrt (max [my-group] of people + 1))
report patch
(round ((world-width / side) * (my-group mod side)
+ min-pxcor + int (world-width / (side * 2))))
(round ((world-height / side) * int (my-group / side)
+ min-pycor + int (world-height / (side * 2))))
end
```

```
to assign-by-size
ask people [set my-group -1]
let unassigned people
let current 0
while [any? Unassigned]
[
ask n-of (min(list group-size (count unassigned)))
  unassigned
[set my-group current]
set current current + 1
set unassigned unassigned with [my-group = -1]
]
end

to paint-in-radius
ask people with [color = cyan]
[paint-agents patches in-radius 3]
ask people with [color = red]
[paint-agents patches in-radius 3]
end

to paint-agents [agents]
ask people with [color = cyan] [set pcolor cyan]
ask people with [color = red] [set pcolor red]
end

to eat
ask people [if pcolor = yellow [set pcolor black set
  energy (energy + 10)]]
end

to regrow-grass
ask patches with [pcolor = black] [if random 100 < 3 [set
  pcolor yellow]]
ask patches with [pcolor = cyan] [if random 25 < 3 [set
  pcolor yellow]]
ask patches with [pcolor = red] [if random 25 < 3 [set
  pcolor yellow]]
end

to setup-plots
update-cyan-neighborhood-plot
end
```

```
to update-plots
  update-cyan-neighborhood-plot
end

to update-cyan-neighborhood-plot
  set-current-plot "Person Centered Planning"
  set-current-plot-pen "cyan patches"
  plot count patches with [pcolor = cyan]
  set-current-plot-pen "red patches"
  plot count patches with [pcolor = red]
end
```

Appendix C

Example of an Agent-Based Model Report

Based on Gilbert's recommendations (2008), it is suggested that the dissemination of ABMs take the following format, which uses the materials developed for the modified Example 2. The abstract, introduction, literature review, and methods sections will appear as they typically would in American Psychological Association (APA) style. The material below only covers those areas that will appear different from a standard APA manuscript.

Statement of Regularities

This complexity model assumes that a random pattern of residential locations indicates community inclusion, as these persons with a disability established support systems and became randomly dispersed in the community. The hypothesis for the person-centered planning complexity model is that individual support and encouragement of persons with disabilities is essential to community inclusion, and that becomes evident through the emergence of agent groups, which indicate a reduction in spatially isolated concentrations of agents with disabilities.

Description of Agent-Based Model to Community Inclusion

In evaluating the inclusion of the people with disabilities (the agents), we used five explanatory variables. These were (1) the degree of involvement by families and friends in the planning process, (2) the number of unrelated persons with whom the individual resided, 3) the proportion of earned income to total income, (4) the level of disability, and (5) the level of mobility. The methods used in the evaluation involved a sample (n = 150) that included data on these five variables. The gender ratio of the samples were consistent with the gender ratio of the entire population.

The spatial autocorrelation and regression analysis included collecting data on the individual consumer level, mapping the data, assessing spatial randomness using Moran's I for each explanatory variable, creating local indicator of special associations for regression analysis, performing regression of the five explanatory variables, and assessing the influence of control variables in regression procedures. Data was collected from agency records and annual planning meetings for individuals. Geography of individuals was represented in a two-dimensional space, longitude and latitude were plotted on *Mapinfo* software, and ten addresses and coordinates were checked on a map to insure accuracy. The agent-based complexity model allowed the role of person-centered planning in community inclusion to be evaluated. To demonstrate how a complexity model can evaluate person-centered planning, the appendix provides the computer code needed to create a complex adaptive system as an agent-based model. Illustrations from that agent-based model are provided below. In the model, the agents are designated by different colors.

To illustrate the role of boundaries on a community, all agents are instructed to form groups or neighborhoods with other agents. The number of groups the agents form can be changed by the evaluator using the *group-size* slide bar and the *assign-by-group* button. Cyan and red colored agents represent people with disabilities. For these agents, having a disability limits their movement within the model. However, cyan agents can increase their mobility by organizing in groups containing five or more green agents. Green agents represent people without disabilities and represent the component of attraction in complex systems.

Self-organization is demonstrated by the cyan and red agents organizing, based on the information they receive and transmit to their allies. Allies are green agents that are linked to cyan agents. The link appears as a line connecting the agents. Red agents serve as the model's control population, and they are not linked to any agents and do not receive benefits from being near green agents. Cyan and red agents are given the order to change the color of their surroundings when they are in proximity to five or more green agents. By changing the color of their surroundings, the model graphs the number of cyan and red agents organizing with green agents, this serves as feedback for the program evaluator. As the graphs in the results section show, cyan agents organize with green agents in higher numbers than red agents do; this is the emergent behavior (see Figure 7.1 in chapter 7 as example).

Parameters of the Model

In creating the model, 150 agents were created; of these 150, 12 agents were red control agents and 12 were cyan agents. The numbers of agents with disabilities was set at 24 to provide a population percentage similar to the number of people with disabilities in the general population. Of the 12 cyan agents, 10 were linked to varying numbers of green agents that represented allies. Numbers of allies ranged from 0 to 3 per cyan agent; and 2 cyan agents were not linked to any green agents. The numbers were based on the number of allies a person with disabilities may have involved in their person-centered planning. Of the 126 green agents, 22 were randomly linked to the 10 cyan agents. In linking green and cyan agents, they were able to influence one another's movements throughout the model in the same manner that the decisions allies and people with disabilities influence actions. To replicate the relationships among allies, community members and people with disabilities (cyan and green agents) were incentivized to interact through providing agents with additional energy for movement within the model.

Cyan agents were given instructions to increase their energy level + 10 whenever they were around five or more green agents. Green agents were instructed to increase their energy level + 5 when around three or more cyan agents. The difference between energy increases was to equalize the agents' energy level at 20, as green agents started with energy of 15, and cyan agents started with energy of 10. Energy provided the simplest commodity in the model to emphasize, because of the agents' dependence on sufficient levels of energy to interact within the community.

Green, red, and cyan agents were directed to form groups with group size determined by the evaluator. Without evaluator input on the size of groups, the agents will form one large group in the center of the model. This outcome makes it impossible to evaluate the effectiveness of person-centered planning. The model was tested at group sizes of 10 agents to provide large enough groups for a variety of different access to groups by the agents.

In this model, the red and cyan agents reported their community integration to the evaluator through changing the color of surrounding patches when 5 or more green agents were present. The number of patches being changed is recorded on a graph that charts the number of patches over time. The greater the number of patches, the larger the population of agents that grouped with green agents and integrated into the community.

Results

In all models, the results were similar. As the agents sought out groups to join, both red and cyan agents were near the largest number of green agents at approximately 15 iterations. The numbers for the red agents began to steadily drop off after 15 iterations. The cyan agents' numbers, however, remained at the same level with some fluctuations. Based on these results it appears that agents with allies in the community experience greater community inclusion than agents without allies. The results of several models were shown in chapter 7 (see Figure 7.2). The greater degree of community inclusion among cyan agents and red agents is the result of the community links between cyan agents and green agents, as well as the reciprocal energy relationship between the cyan and green agents.

Discussion

Researchers and program evaluators may explore the use of agent-based modeling (ABM) for creating predictive simulations of social service phenomena. ABM applies a bottom-up approach that accounts for individual agent behavior, rather than the traditional top–down testing of models. It provides a sensitive method for investigating individual responses to social interventions. Investigating the properties of robustness (resiliency), scalability in generalist social work practice (e.g., use of goals and objectives at both the individual client and program levels), and the diversity of agents (Miller & Page, 2007) appear to be key research foci for social work researchers to develop.

The results consistently demonstrated that agents with allies experienced a greater degree of community inclusion. These findings are reinforced by the earlier work of Wolf-Branigin, Leroy, & Miller (2001) that found person-center planning and self-organizing reduces barriers to community inclusion for people with disabilities. A challenge in creating the person-centered planning complexity model was identifying the appropriate NetLogo procedures to simulate the benefits of community inclusion. Using energy as a reciprocal benefit of community inclusion may not have been necessary for agents. The energy requirements for mobility among all agents were low enough that additional energy may not have been needed for participation in the model. Future versions of the person-centered planning model should focus on manipulating the energy and mobility of agents to determine how energy level affects agent interaction and inclusion.

The primary disadvantages include having difficulty creating multi-agent models for simulating phenomena, but will be a vital line of work for future researchers. Given the problems social program managers encounter when adopting simple inferential statistics, applying agent-based modeling may be a difficult task.

This evaluation analyzed housing patterns of persons with an intellectual or developmental disability. This intellectual and developmental disability application demonstrates that the use of feedback in person-centered planning assists persons to become fully participating citizens in their communities. Person-centered planning, a technique that individuals with disabilities and their supporters use to think about and plan for the future, emerged from a concern that professionals working in government-funded organizations were not providing supports that people value as they planned their futures (LeRoy, Wolf-Branigin, Wolf-Branigin, Israel, Kulik, 2007). In this example, person-centered planning methodologies included self-organizing clusters of supporting individuals representing various aspects of the lives of persons with disabilities. These individuals supported and encouraged persons with disabilities as an alternative to the government-funded professional human service systems.

This application focused on the self-organizing that leads to attraction at the micro-level, with progress expected at interpersonal levels rather than macro (systems) levels. Using feedback affected several life domains, including housing, education, employment, health, and social services.

Reducing barriers within the individual's environment was essential to improving social life, encouraging inclusion, and reducing spatially isolated concentrations for people with limited financial resources.

Conclusions and Implications for Social Work.

Challenges exist when applying CAS to measure the collective behavior of agents rather than the simple aggregated outcomes of program participants. These problems must address defining the boundaries of models, verifying the reliability and validity of models, keeping the model agent-based, and deciding when a CAS approach best fits (Epstein, 2006). Evaluators should integrate available statistical and mathematical tools (e.g., social network analysis, game theory) with the new media into a cohesive toolbox and model. New media methods (e.g., social networking) provide promising platforms for evaluation communities to self-organize, problem solve, and facilitate multidisciplinary collaboration (Hollingshead & Contractor, 2006).

Several aspects of complexity theory and ABM show promising fields of study for social work. These include complex networks, pattern repetition through fractal analysis, the discovery of power laws and scalability (Barabasi, 2002), bursts of activity in daily life (Barabasi, 2010), and the wisdom of groups and their related behaviors (Surowiecki, 2004). Those seeking a more detailed account of complex systems theory and its antecedents are referred to Gell-Mann (1994), Johnson (2009), or Mitchell (2009).

Appendix D

Additional Resources

Books

These books offer an introduction to complexity theory and its application across a vast spectrum.

- Gilbert, N. (2008). *Agent based modeling.* Los Angeles: Sage. This brief book provides a dense overview, with a worked example using Net Logo software.
- Hudson, C. (2010). *Complex systems and human behavior.* Chicago: Lyceum. Using complexity theory orientation within the social work literature, this is a very detailed and excellent book, focusing on human behavior in the social environment courses.
- Johnson, N. (2009). *Simple complexity: A clear guide to complexity theory.* Oxford, England: Oxford University Press. This well-written book gives the reader an excellent primer on complexity.
- Miller, J. H., & Page, S. E. (2007). *Complex adaptive systems: An introduction to computational models of social life.* Princeton, NJ: Princeton University Press. This book suggests a useful overview for computational complexity in social sciences; however, it is technical.
- Mitchell, M. (2009). *Complexity: A guided tour.* New York: Oxford University Press. This is an excellent primer to complex systems.

- Westley, F., Zimmerman, B., & Patton, M. Q. (2006). *Getting to maybe: How the world is changed*, Toronto: Random House Canada. Oriented toward social innovation and inspiring social change with a nontechnical approach, this book provides a strong link to how complexity theory underlies social change efforts.

Journals on Complexity, Agent-Based Modeling, and Social Innovation

- E: CO Emergence: Complexity & Organization (http://emergentpublications.com)
- Innovations (http://www.mitpressjournals.org/loi/itgg)
- Stanford Social Innovation Review (http://www.ssireview.org)

Institutes and Centers

- George Mason University—Center for Social Complexity at Chap. 7 Rev.docx (http://socialcomplexity.gmu.edu)
- Santa Fe Institute (http://www.santafe.edu)
- University of Michigan (http://www.cscs.umich.edu)

Centers for Social Innovation

- The Centre for Social Innovation—Toronto (http://www.socialinnovation.ca)
- Center for Social Entrepreneurship at George Mason University (http://www.masoninnovation.org/)
- Plexus Institute (http://www.plexusinstitute.org)
- The Roosevelt Institute (http://www.rooseveltinstitute.org)
- Skoll Social Edge (http://www.socialedge.org)
- Stanford University Graduate Business School's Center for Social Innovation (http://www.gsb.stanford.edu/csi/).

Simulation Software

- NetLogo (http://ccl.northwestern.edu/netlogo/) and its user groups.

- New Media Consortium (http://www.nmc.org/) provides educators with information on current and emerging technology and techniques for application.

Social Network Analysis Software

Four software packages are available that build upon one another. The base program is UCINET. (Each of these programs are free or of minimal cost.)

- UCINET: used for data entry/descriptive
- NETDRAW: used to visualize and draw a network
- Pajek: used for data management and visualization
- qStOCNET: used for advanced and inferential analyses

Videos

- NovaNow, Emergence (2007) (http://www.pbs.org/wgbh/nova/nature/emergence.html)
- Videos from Cristobol VilaEsfahan Architecture Animation: (http://www.youtube.com/watch?v=jc9t50C7WOU).
- Nature by Numbers: (http://www.youtube.com/watch?v=kkGeOWYOFoA&feature=related).

Websites

- For those interested in useful information on applied and theoretical mathematics on complexity theory, please visit the Wolfram Mathematics site (http://mathworld.wolfram.com/).
- If you are seeking to locate colleagues with a shared interest in technology and human services, visit the Human Service Information Technical Applications website (HUSITA) (http://www.husita.org/).
- For a general science magazine that applies complexity across disciplines, please see *Seed* Magazine (http://www.seedmagazine.com) It has a strong complex systems orientation and addresses issues from a broad range of disciplines, including the social sciences.

- Community mapping provides a useful tool for understanding the resources available in a defined community. It can also be used for spatial analysis and GIS. For more on this useful tool, visit PolicyLink—Community Mapping (http://policylink.info/EDTK/Mapping/How.html)

Assistance with Agent-Based Modeling

- NetLogo Users Group (http://groups.yahoo.com/group/netlogo-users/) includes both expert and novice users of NetLogo who will assist in answering a range of questions.
- NetLogo Educators Group (http://groups.yahoo.com/group/netlogo-educators/), similar to the users group, supports questions from instructors seeking assistance on classroom-based projects.Curricula and classroom resources (http://ccl.northwestern.edu/#Curriculum) from the Center for Connected Learning and Computer-Based Modeling, Northwestern University.
- NetLogoWiki (http://www.turtlezero.com/wiki/doku.php) from TurtleZero.com.

Glossary

Agent-based modeling (ABM) A computational modeling method that assumes a bottom–up approach by using data from agents (individuals, families, or groups), as opposed to a top–down structure.

Agents The persons, families, or groups (units of analysis) within complex systems, and more specifically, agent-based models. Agents operate within a defined space. This space allows for the observation of local phenomena, such as the search for resources, the effect of relative scarcity, and competition within confined spaces.

Boolean logic Similar to algebra, this branch of mathematics uses formulas that apply the constants "0" and "1" rather than numbers. These values should not be viewed as numbers, but instead as "yes/no" or "on/off".

Boundaries The limits placed on a complex system in order to keep the system maintained. In social service applications, these may range from social legislation, geographic region, or the limits placed on the available choices of agents.

Catastrophe theory Related to chaos theory, this branch of mathematics studies dynamical systems and is concerned with how small changes within a system can produce large effects.

Cellular automata The successive generation from the agents' actions that simulate or generate what we expect to observe in the model.

Chaos theory Often confused with complexity theory, chaos theory refers to sensitivity to initial conditions, where small effects can lead to major changes in a dynamical system.

Complex adaptive systems (CAS) Complex systems in which the system itself adapts to changing conditions.

Complexity theory This emerging paradigm in the physical and social sciences seeks to understand how agents self-organize, and then how they continually use feedback to produce an emergent behavior.

Complex systems The settings in which complexity is exhibited. Complex systems are comprised of a series of components, including agents, heterogeneity, self-organization, feedback, and an emergent behavior.

Computation theory The branch of mathematics that addresses how efficiently problems can be solved using an allowable set of operations. This occurs by using an algorithm (a limited number of steps). It provides a valuable bottom–up framework that accounts for individual client (agent) behavior, resulting in larger patterns than in a top–down approach for the testing of models.

Convergence In complexity theory this refers to the idea that some functions and sequences approach a limit under certain conditions. It may also refer to a sequence of adaptations coming to the same conclusion, no matter what order they occur in.

Cybernetics Formally the study of communication and control, but as applied to social work, cybernetics may be seen as the use of feedback by groups and organizations for the purpose of learning and continual quality improvement.

Description length The minimum amount of data that can communicate the essential information.

Decision theory This branch of research, based on game theory, studies the values, uncertainties, and other issues related to how individuals, groups, or organizations make a decision, the reasons behind the decision, and the best or optimal decision that results.

Developmental evaluation An evaluation method that attempts to find order out of what emerges from a social service intervention by understanding the interdependencies and innovations as they occur.

Diverse heuristics Represents the different and unique problem-solving skill sets that agents have.

Diverse perspectives These represent the different backgrounds and experiences of individual agents. These diverse experiences assist in garnering broader ideas that contribute to problem solving.

Dynamical systems theory Linked to chaos theory, this branch of applied mathematics asks whether a system will settle down into a steady state.

Ecosystems theory An extension of (general) systems theory, this theory looks beyond a person's sphere to focus on the intersection of the person's system and the larger environment. The person and the environment react to each other.

Edge of chaos Because social service systems are dynamic, some instability continually occurs; it is at the edge of this chaos that innovation occurs. In a thoughtful process, it involves the combining and winnowing of ideas.

Effective complexity Represents the length of nonrandom information, or measures the information content of the regularities in a system.

Emergence/emergent behavior The structures and functions that arise from the interactions of agents.

Entanglement Refers to the interdependencies that result in complex systems and social networks. This entanglement can have both positive and negative consequences as a positive flow of information or as a contagion.

Evolutionary computation This field, related to artificial intelligence, uses an iterative process to simulate population development or growth. Agent-based modeling provides a platform for simulating such populations.

Feedback Information provided by the system that is received by the system and is used for improvement.

Force field analysis Developed by Kurt Lewin, this technique creates a process for problem solving and managing change. It is based on two assumptions: in every situation there are forces driving change and forces resisting change, and an emphasis on reducing resisting forces is more efficient than increasing the driving forces.

General systems theory Developed by von Bertalanffy, this theory describes the functioning of all living systems by understanding that the functioning of one system affects other systems connected to it.

Groupthink This problem occurs when groups of teams lack diversity of thought and, therefore, make decisions to reach consensus that avoid potential conflict.

In silico Refers to something carried out through computer simulation.

Interconnectedness The assumption that all agents are in one way or another connected to all other agents. These interconnections produce influences on how other agents act.

Kolmogorov complexity A basis of computational theory, this definition of complexity refers to the minimum length of a computational program, written in the description language, which produces the desired sequence of symbols.

Lattice data Spatial data, in which each cell has eight surrounding cells: one immediately above, one immediately below, one to either side, and four on the diagonal. Understanding lattice data plays a prominent role in agent-based models because of how simple rules will affect areas (cells) surrounding the agents.

Meme A unit of social information, such as a belief, that is transmitted or spread to agents. These memes can replicate and can be the information transmitted in networks.

Neural networks Referred to originally as a network or circuit of biological neurons, but more recently adopted as a framework for the study of artificial and statistical neural networks.

Niche construction The study of how agents (represented as clients) alter their environment by using feedback to improve the likelihood for survival; appears to be a promising construct for inquiry into this transitional phase.

Nonlinearity Seeks to account for more than just simple cause-and-effect when investigating social service phenomena, using methods such as spatial analysis, social network analysis, and agent-based modeling. Nonlinearity occurs when small initial changes produce large effects.

Power laws The mathematical relationship between two quantities, where the frequency of an event varies in relation to some characteristic of that event (e.g. size). The resulting frequency follows a power law. Power laws are found frequently in scale-free networks.

Random graphs A model for a network in which some parameters, such as edges or nodes, take fixed values, but are random otherwise.

Self-organizing behavior The component of complex systems theory that serves as a magnet. It is what draws agents with similar interests or concerns together to act upon an issue.

Self-similarity Seen in fractals, this is the repeating patterns that arise at different levels of observation. In social work, we may see this in writing goals or objectives, whether for an individual, a family unit, or a program evaluation.

Sensitivity to initial conditions Assumes that the initial state of a complex system has a large influence on how the system will develop.

Simple rules Based on some preference, the decisions made by agents at the individual level, which in turn shape the emergent behavior.

Simulate Refers to the ability to develop and generate a model using computational methods, such as agent-based modeling.

Small-world networks In social network analysis, a type of network in which most nodes (agents) are not neighbors of one another, but most nodes can be reached from every other node by following only a few links.

Social innovation Refers to ideas, strategies, concepts, and organizations that meet diverse social needs and that extend and strengthens society. These might range from micro-financing, working conditions, or education reform to community development and health.

Social network analysis The quantitative study of social behavior and the influences that individuals and groups have on others who are linked together. There are two broad categories: egocentric and whole networks.

Spatial autocorrelation A specific application of spatial analysis that refers to the extent to which the occurrence of an event in one area is influenced by the distribution of similar features in a neighboring area.

Spatial and/or geographic methods The research and statistical methods in which location provides an effect.

Statistical complexity Suggests a definition of complexity whereby that an algorithm is used to classify existing data so that it can be generated to produce patterns that are similar to the original data.

Unintended consequences Refers to the inability to predict all effects resulting from an intervention. Based on the concept of quantum mechanics, the unpredicted effects are unintended consequences.

Validation In agent-based modeling, this refers to the developed model being tested and validated to assure that it represents what it purports to represent.

Verification Once an agent-based model is developed, it needs to be debugged and verified. This is the process of verifying that the model satisfies what it was intended to do.

Wicked questions Problems that cannot be answered with traditional analytic approaches; such questions typically involve a high level of uncertainty.

Wisdom of crowds Implies that the typical (average) response from a group of individuals will, in most instances, generate a reasonable estimate of phenomena.

Notes

Chapter 1

[1] The terms "predict" and "forecast" are used interchangeably throughout this text. In discussing this matter with a few developers of agent-based models, they preferred the term forecast (as in weather forecasting).

[2] A page or two was planned on explaining quantum mechanics, but recently, while talking with a physicist during a baseball game, I realized that my understanding of the topic was, to say the least, minimal. Therefore, that has been left out of the book. Instead you are referred to the numerous online sources for a better understanding.

[3] The examples in this book were intentionally oriented toward evaluation and research with persons with disabilities. This occurred because during the past four decades, this group and their supporters have aimed to be fully included members of society, focusing on interconnectedness, community inclusion, and self-determination.

Chapter 2

[1] After attending a discussion between Supreme Court Justice Ruth Bader Ginsburg and National Public Radio's Nina Totenberg, it became apparent to me that throughout American history, the Supreme Court has functioned as a complex system, given that the agenda percolates up to the court from lower court decisions and, over time, decisions change. often based on past dissenting opinions.

Chapter 3

[1] As an MSW student in the late 1970s, I had Wilbur Cohen (aka the father of Social Security) as a professor for social policy. On more than one occasion he stated, "Programs for the poor are poor programs." His statement in effect encourages interconnectedness across income groups.

[2] Because many readers will be doctoral students in the early phases of thinking and preparing their dissertation work, please be aware that this phase of your education can influence your agenda strongly in the short- and long-term. Choosing a topic and method of greatest interest to you should really make your future academic career more productive.

Chapter 4

[1] In the summer of 2007, I had the pleasure of meeting with Harold Morowitz, Clarence Robinson Professor of Natural Philosophy at George Mason University, and one of the founders of the Santa Fe Institute. The meeting was to discuss shifting the application of complexity theory within social work beyond metaphorical applications. He convinced me that all this was fine, but in the end, all is metaphorical anyway.

[2] Those seeking detailed accounts on applying these advanced statistical methods are advised to consult the plethora of strong texts on the respective topic. Those seeking information on structural equation modeling, please see Bollen (1989), for hierarchical linear modeling see Bryk and Raudenbush (1992), and for social network analysis see Wasserman and Faust (1994).

[3] My experience has been that taking a specific course in one of the advanced methods (e.g., spatial analysis, HLM, social network analysis) is a great way for really getting the background, skills, and feel for the data analysis. I recommend courses such as those provided through other departments within your university or the Summer Institute on Advanced Quantitative Methods at the Interuniversity Consortium for Political and Social Research.

Chapter 5

[1] The social program evaluations used in this chapter come from several studies that colleagues and I completed over the past decade. Minor changes were included in an attempt to have the materials more closely align with the concepts discussed in the chapter.

Chapter 6

[1] This example of a model evolved from my 1999 dissertation work. Jakob Klaus, a graduate research assistant at the time of this writing, was instrumental in developing the model.

Chapter 7

[1] This chapter was coauthored with Jakob Klaus, who was instrumental in developing the coding for the models.
[2] At the time this book was written, social-work-oriented agent-based models were not published in social work journals, but rather in broader social science journals, nor were the models solely developed by social workers. An objective of mine in developing this book is that social workers gain the requisite knowledge to develop the models.

Chapter 8

[1] As noted by Dr. Udaya Sharma, a social innovator from Katmandu Nepal, a preference for micro grants rather than micro loans appears to be gaining momentum as an alternative to the abuses arising from micro lending.
[2] Faculty often peruse potential books and other instructional materials for their upcoming social work courses. I recently adopted a new text for an MSW social program evaluation class. While I liked the book and found the price right for students, a few of the students thought the author was just too excited about the topic. While finding complexity extremely useful, I hope not to relay the same message.

References

Aaker, J., & Smith, A. (2010). *The dragonfly effect: Quick, effective, and powerful ways to use social media to drive social change*. San Francisco: Jossey-Bass.

Adams, K. B., Matto, H. C., & LeCroy, C. W. (2009). Limitations of evidence-based practice for social work education: Unpacking the complexity. *Journal of Social Work Education, 45*(2), 165–186.

Agar, M. (1999). Complexity theory: An exploration and overview. *Field Methods, 11*, 99–120.

Alemi, F., Stephens, R., Llorens, S., Schaefer, D., Nemes, S., & Arendt, R. (2003). The Orientation of Social Support measure. *Addictive Behaviors, 28*, 1285–1298.

Alexander, B. (2009). A web game for predicting some futures: Exploring the wisdom of crowds. *EDUCAUSE Review, 44*(3). Retrieved January 4, 2011, from http://www.educause.edu/EDUCAUSE+Review/EDUCAUSEReviewMagazineVolume44/AWebGameforPredictingSomeFutur/171494.

Alinsky, S. (1971). *Rules for radicals: A pragmatic primer for realistic radicals*. New York: Random House.

Andreae, D. (2011). General systems theory: Contributions to social work theory and practice. In F. J. Turner (Ed.), *Social work treatment: Interlocking approaches* (5th ed., pp. 242–254). New York: Oxford University Press.

Andrews, A. B., Motes, P. S., Floyd, A. G., Flerx, V. C., & Fede, A. L. (2005). Building evaluation capacity in community-based organizations: Reflections of an empowerment evaluation team. *Journal of Community Practice, 13*(4), 85–104. doi: 10.1300/J125v13n4_06

Anselin, L., Florax, R., & Rey, S. (2004). *Advances in spatial econometrics. Methodology, tools, and applications*. Berlin: Springer-Verlag.

Axelrod, R. (1984). *The evolution of cooperation* (pp. 109–168). Jackson, TN: Basic Books.

Axelrod, R. (1997). *The Complexity of Cooperation: Agent-based Models of Competition and Collaboration*, Princeton, NJ: Princeton University Press.

Axinn, J., & Stern, M. J. (2008). *Social welfare: A history of the American response to need* (7th ed). Boston: Allyn & Bacon.

Bailey, T., & Gatrell, A. (1995). *Interactive Spatial Data Analysis*. Essex, UK: Longman.

Barabasi, A. L. (2002). *Linked: The new science of networks*. Cambridge, MA: Perseus.

Barabasi, A. L. (2010). *Bursts: The hidden pattern behind everything we do*. New York: Dutton.

Bednar, J. (2009). *The robust federation: Principles of design*. Cambridge, UK: Cambridge University Press.

Bettencourt, L., & West, G. (2010). A unified theory of urban living. *Nature, 467*, 912–913. doi: 10.1038/467912a

Bliss, J. R., Gillespie, D. F., & Gongaware, N. K. (2010). Dynamics of caseworker turnover and clinical knowledge. *Administration in Social Work, 34*, 4–26. doi: 10.1080/03634100903172992

Bloom, M., Fischer, J., & Orme, J. G. (2006). *Evaluating practice: Guidelines for the accountable professional* (5th ed). Boston: Allyn & Bacon.

Bolland, K., & Atherton, C. (1999). Chaos theory: An alternative approach to social work practice and research. *Families in Society: The Journal of Contemporary Human Services, 80*(4), 367–373.

Bollen, K. A. (1989). *Structural equations with latent variables*. New York: Wiley.

Braddock, D. (2002). *Disability at the dawn of the 21st century and the state of the States*. Washington, DC: American Association on Mental Retardation.

Bronfenbrenner, U. (1994). Ecological models of human development. In *International Encyclopedia of Education* (2nd ed., Vol. 3, pp. 1643–1647). London: Elsevier.

Brooks, D. (2011). *The social animal: The hidden sources of love, character, and achievement*. New York: Random House.

Bryk, A. S., & Raudenbush, S. W. (1992). *Hierarchical linear models*. Newbury Park, CA: Sage.

Burkardt, J., McGavock, A., & Nelson, C. (2002). *Improving public transit options for older persons*. Washington, DC: TCRP, Transportation Research Board of the National Academies.

Burton, J., & van den Broek, D. (2008). Accountable and countable: Information management systems and the bureaucratization of social work. *British Journal of Social Work, 38*, 493–506.

Campbell, S. L. (2011). Chaos theory and social work treatment. In F. J. Turner (Ed.), *Social work treatment: Interlocking approaches* (5th ed., pp. 48–57). New York: Oxford University Press.
CARF, The Rehabilitation Accreditation Commission (2010). *Employment and community support accreditation standards*. Tucson, AZ: CARF.
Castells, M. (2004). *The network society: A cross-cultural perspective*. Northampton, MA: Edward Elgar.
Casti, J., & DePauli, W. (2000). *Godel: A life of logic* (pp. 166–190). Cambridge, MA: Perseus Publishing.
Chou, Y.-H. (1997). *Exploring spatial analysis in geographical information systems*. Santa Fe, NM: Onward Press.
Christakis, N. A., & Fowler, J. H. (2009). *Connected: The surprising power of social networks and how they shape our lives*. New York: Little, Brown and Company.
Clauset, A., Shalizi, C. R., & Newman, M. E. J. (2007). Power-law distributions in empirical data. *Journal of Conflict Resolution, 51*(1), 58–88.
Coghlan, D., & Brannick, T. (2005). *Doing action research in your own organization*. London: Sage.
Cournoyer, B. (2004). *The evidence-based social work skills book*. Boston: Allyn and Bacon.
Crain & Associates, Inc. (1998.) *Using public transportation to reduce the economic, social and human costs of personal immobility*. Washington, DC: TCRP, Transportation Research Board of the National Academies. Retrieved October 24, 2007, from http://www.nap.edu/catalog.php?record_id=9438#toc.
Cressie, N. (1993). *Statistics for spatial data*. New York: Wiley.
Creswell, J. (2003). *Research design: Qualitative, quantitative, and mixed model approaches* (2nd ed.). Thousand Oaks, CA: Sage.
Cronbach, L. (1988). Playing chess with chaos. *Educational Researcher, 17*(6), 46–49.
Crutchfield, J. P., & Young, K. (1989). Inferring statistical complexity. *Physical Review Letters, 63*(2), 105–108.
Czarniawska, B. (2004). *Narratives in social science research*. London: Sage.
Deng. K., & Chu, T. (2011). Action being character: A promising perspective on the solution concept of game theory. *PLoS ONE* 6(5): e19014. doi:10.1371/journal.pone.0019014
De Tocqueville, A. (1840). *Democracy in America*. New York: J. & H. G. Langley.
Dijksterhuis, A., & Nordgren L. F. (2006). A theory of unconscious thought. *Perspectives on Psychological Science, 1*, 95–180.
Durkheim, E. (1951). *Suicide: A study in sociology*. New York: Free Press.
Eichler, M. (2007). *Consensus organizing: Building communities of mutual self-interest*. Thousand Oaks, CA: Sage.

Electronic Arts, Inc. (2007). *SimCity Societies*. Redwood City, CA: Tilted Game entertainment.

Epperson, B., & Li, T. (1996). Measurement of genetic structure within populations using Moran's spatial autocorrelation statistics. *Proceedings of the National Academy of Sciences*, 93(19), 10,528–10,532.

Epstein, J. M., & Axtell, R. L. (1996). *Growing artificial societies: Social science from the bottom up*. Cambridge, MA: MIT Press.

Epstein, J. M. (1999). Agent-based computational models and generative social science. *Complexity*, 4(5). 41–60.

Epstein, J. M. (2006). *Generative social science: Studies in agent-based computational modeling*. Princeton, NJ: Princeton University Press.

ESPA (2007). *Introduction to travel training course curriculum*. Washington, DC: Easter Seals Project Action.

Farmer, R. L. (2009). *Neuroscience and social work practice: The missing link*. Los Angeles: Sage.

Felix-Geyer, R. F., & van der Zouwen, J. (2001) *Sociocybernetics: Complexity, autopoiesis, and observation of social systems*, Santa Barbara, CA: Greenwood Publishing Group.

Ferenstein, G. (2011, February 20). How tech giants came to rule the world by sharing. *The Washington Post*, pp. G1 & G4.

Flack, J. C., Girvan, M., de Waal, F., & Krakauer, D. C. (2006). Policing stabilizes construction of social niches in primates. *Nature*, 439(7075), 426–429.

Fogel, R. W. (2000). *The Fourth Great Awakening and the future of egalitarianism*. Chicago: University of Chicago Press.

Folke, C. (2010). On resilience. *Seedmagazine.com*. Retrieved January 5, 2011, from http://seedmagazine.com/content/article/on_resilience/.

Freire, P. (1994). *Pedagogy of hope: Reliving pedagogy of the oppressed*. New York: Continuum.

Gans, H. J. (2011). Public presence and social science. *Seedmagazine.com*. Retrieved February 7, 2011, from http://seedmagazine.com/content/article/on_public_presence_and_social_science/.

Gell-Mann, M. (1994). *The quark and the jaguar: Adventures in the simple and the complex*. New York: W. H. Freeman and Company.

Gell-Mann, M., & Lloyd, S. (1996). Information measures, effective complexity, and total information. *Complexity*, 2(1), 44–52.

Germain, C., & Gitterman, A. (1980). *The life model of social work practice*. New York: Columbia University Press.

Gettis, A. (1991). Spatial interaction and spatial autocorrelation; A cross-product approach. *Environment and Planning A*, 23, 1269–1277.

Gilbert, N. (2008). *Agent based modeling*. Los Angeles: Sage.

Gladwell, M. (2000). *The tipping point: How little things can make a big difference*. New York: Little Brown.

Gleick, J. (1987). *Chaos: Making a new science*. New York: Viking.

Gleick, J. (2011). *The information: A history, a theory, a flood*. New York: Pantheon Books.

Goldin, I. (2010). On systemic risk. *Seedmagizine.com*. Retrieved January 4, 2011, from http://seedmagazine.com/content/print/on_systemic_risk/.

Gorman, D., Mezic, J., Mezic, I., & Gruenewald, P. (2006). Agent-based modeling of,drinking behavior: A preliminary model and potential applications to theory and practice. *American Journal of Public Health*, 96(11), 2055–2060.

Graham, R. J. (1993). Decoding teaching: The rhetoric and politics of narrative form. *Journal of Natural Inquiry*, 8(1), 300–37.

Greene, R. R. (2007). *Social work practice: A risk and resilience perspective*. Belmont, CA: Brooks/Cole.

Grimm, V., Revilla, E., Berger, U., Jeltsch, F., Mooij, W., Railsback, S., et al. (2005). Pattern-oriented modeling of agent-based complex systems: Lessons from ecology. *Science*, 310, 987–991.

Groce, M. (1996). An introduction to travel training. *NICHY*, 9, June 1996, 2–5.

Guggenheim, C. (1999). *Life in the Shadows: The emergence of mental retardation into public awareness* [Documentary film]. Washington, DC: Joseph P. Kennedy Jr. Foundation.

Halmi, A. (2003). Chaos and non-linear dynamics: New methodological approaches in the social sciences and social work practice. *International Social Work*, 46(1), 83–101.

Hamil, L., & Gilbert, N. (2010). Simulating large social networks in agent-based models: A social circle model, *E: CO Emergence: Complexity & Organization*, 12(4), 78–94.

Hasenfeld, Y. (2010). *Human services as complex organizations* (2nd ed). Los Angeles: Sage.

Hillier, A. (2007). Why social work needs mapping. *Journal of Social Work Education*, 43(2), 205–221.

Holling, C. S. (1973). Resilience and stability of ecological systems. *Annual Review of Ecology and Systematics*, 4, 1–23.

Hollingshead, A., & Contractor, N. (2006). New media and small group organizing. In L. Lievrouw & S. Livingstone (Eds.), *The handbook of new media* (pp. 114–133). London: Sage.

Holland, J. H. (1975) *Adaptation in natural and artificial systems*. Cambridge, MA: MIT Press.

Holland, J. H. (1998). *Emergency from chaos to order*. Reading, MA: Helix Books.

Homan, M. S. (2011). *Promoting community change: Making it happen in the real world* (5th ed). Belmont, CA: Brooks Cole.

Hudson, C. G. (2000). At the edge of chaos: A new paradigm for social work? *Journal of Social Work Education, 36*(2), 215–230.

Hudson, C. G. (2004). The dynamics of self-organization: Neglected dimensions. *Journal of Human Behavior in the Social Environment, 10*(4), 17–37.

Hudson, C. (2010). *Complex systems and human behavior.* Chicago: Lyceum.

Husock, H. (1992). Bringing back the settlement house. *Public Interest, 109,* 53–72.

Iannuzziello, A. (2001). *Communicating with persons with disabilities in a multimodal transit environment: A synthesis of transit practice.* TCRP, Washington, DC: TCRP, Transportation Research Board of the National Academies.

Institute of Medicine of the National Academies (2006). *Improving the quality of health care for mental and substance-use conditions.* Committee on Crossing the Quality Chasm: Adaptation to Mental Health and Addictive Disorders. Washington, DC: The National Academies Press.

Israel, N., & Wolf-Branigin, M. (2011). Nonlinearity in human service evaluation: A primer on agent based modeling. *Social Work Research, 35*(1), 20–24.

Jacobs, J. (1961). *The death and life of great American cities.* New York: Random House.

Jayprakash, C., Warren, K., Irwin, E., & Chen, K. (2009). The interaction of segregation and suburbanization in an agent-based model of residential location. *Environment and Planning B: Planning and Design, 36,* 989–1007.

Johnson, S. (2002) *Emergence: The connected lives of ants, brains, cities, and software* (3–14). New York: Putnam.

Johnson, N. (2009). *Simple complexity: A clear guide to complexity theory.* Oxford, UK: Oxford University Press.

Kane, M., & Trochim, W. (2007). *Concept mapping for planning and evaluation.* Thousand Oaks, CA: Sage.

Karnani. A. (2011) Microfinance needs regulation. *Stanford Social Innovation Review. 9*(1), 48–53.

Katz, J., and Gartner, W. (1988). Properties of emerging organizations. *Academy of Management Review, 13,* 429–441.

Kaufmann, S. A. (1995). *At home in the universe: The search for the laws of self-organization and complexity.* New York: Oxford University Press.

Kettner, P. M., Moroney, R. M., & Martin, L. L. (2008). *Designing and managing programs: An effectiveness-based approach* (3rd ed). Los Angeles: Sage.

Kelly, K. (2010). *What technology wants.* New York: Viking.

Kennedy, J. F. (1962). *The first international awards for the Joseph P. Kennedy Jr. Foundation* [Speech], 6 December. Statler Hilton Hotel: Washington, DC.

Kennedy, J. F. (1963a). *Proposed measures to combat mental illness and mental retardation* [Speech], 5 February. The White House: Washington, DC.

Kennedy, J. F. (1963b). *Thirteenth annual conference of the National Association for Retarded Children* [Speech], 24 October. Mayflower Hotel: Washington, DC.

Koenig, P. (1980). Indicators of urban Accessibility: Theory and application. *Transportation, 9*, 145–172.

Knoke, D., & Yang, S. (2008). *Social network analysis* (2nd ed). Los Angeles: Sage.

Kuhn, T. S. (1962). *The structure of scientific revolutions*. Chicago: University of Chicago Press.

LeRoy, B., Wolf-Branigin, M., Wolf-Branigin, K., Israel, N., & Kulik, N. (2007). Challenges to the systematic adoption of person-centered planning. *Best Practices in Mental Health: An International Journal, 3*(1), 16–25.

Lee, P. (2004). *Bayesian statistics: An introduction* (3rd ed). London: Arnold.

Lehrer, J. (2010). A physicist solves the city. *New York Times Magazine*, December 17, 2010.

Leroux Miller, K. (2010). *The nonprofit marketing guide: High impact, low-cost ways to build support for your good cause*. San Francisco: Jossey-Bass.

Lewin, K. (1943). Defining the 'field at a given time.' *Psychological Review, 50*, 292–310.

Lewin, R. (1999). *Complexity: Life at the edge of chaos*. London: Phoenix.

Lewis, B., & Bird, B. (2007). *Ratatouille*. USA: Pixar.

Libert, B., & Spector, J. (2008). *We are smarter than me: How to unleash the power of crowds on your business*. Upper Saddle River, NJ: Wharton School Publishing.

Light, P. C. (2011). *Driving social change: How to solve the world's toughest problems*. Hoboken, NJ: Wiley.

Lorenz, E. N. (1963). Deterministic non-periodic flow. *Journal of Atmospheric Science, 20*, 130–141.

Lundblad, K. S. (1995). Jane Addams and social reform: A role model for the 1990s. *Social Work, 40*(5), 661–670.

Malinsky, E., & Lubesky, C. (2011). *Network evaluation: Cultivating healthy networks for social change*. Toronto: Centre for Social Innovation.

Malott, R. (1973). *An introduction to behavior modification*. Kalamazoo, MI: Behaviordelia, Inc.

Manheim, J., Rich, R., Willnat, L., & Brians, C. (2006). *Empirical political analysis: Research methods in political science* (6th ed., pp. 218–229). New York: Pearson Longman.

Mankiewicz, R. (2001). *The story of mathematics*. Princeton, NJ: Princeton University Press.

Maple, F. (1977). *Shared decision-making*. Beverly Hills, CA: Sage.

Martin, D., & Williams, H. (1992). Market-area analysis and availability to primary healthcare. *Environment and Planning A, 24*, 1009–1019.

MASON (2010). *Multi-agent simulator of neighborhoods*. Fairfax, VA: Center for Social Complexity—George Mason University. Retrieved May 4, 2010, from http://cs.gmu.edu/~eclab/projects/mason/.

Matto, H. C., & Strolin-Goltzman, J. (2010). Integrating social neuroscience and social work: Innovations for advancing practice-based research. *Social Work*, 55(2), 147–156.

Mäyrä, F. (2008). *An introduction to game studies: Games in culture* (pp. 13–20). Los Angeles: Sage.

McCaughan, N., & Palmer, B. (1994). *Systems thinking for harassed managers*. London: Karnac.

McCauley, C. (1989). The nature of social influence in groupthink: Compliance and internalization. *Journal of Personality and Social Psychology*. 57(2), 250–260.

McGoldrick, M., Gerson, R., & Petry, S. (2008). *Genograms assessment and interventions* (3rd ed). New York: W.W. Norton & Company.

Mead, M. (1928). *Coming of age in Samoa; A psychological study of primitive youth for Western Civilization*. New York: William Morrow and Company.

Meredith, W., & Tisak, J. (1990). Latent curve analysis. *Psychometrika*, 55(1), 107–122.

Mertler, C. A. (2006). *Action research: Teachers as researchers in the classroom*. Thousand Oaks, CA: Sage.

Micceri, T. (1989). The unicorn, the normal curve, and other improbable creatures. *Psychological Bulletin*, 105(1), 156–166.

Midgley, G. (2006). Systems thinking for evaluation. In B. Williams & I. Imam (Eds), *Systems Concepts in Evaluation: An Expert Anthology* (pp. 11–34). Point Reyes, CA: EdgePress.

Miller, J. H., & Page, S. E. (2007). *Complex adaptive systems: An introduction to computational models of social life*. Princeton, NJ: Princeton University Press.

Mitchell, M. (2009). *Complexity: A guided tour*. New York: Oxford University Press.

Mizrahi, T., & Rosenthal, B. B. (2001). Complexities of coalition building: Leaders' successes, strategies, struggles and solutions. *Social Work*, 46(1) 63–78.

Mondros, J. B., & Wilson, S. M. (1994). *Organizing for power and empowerment*. New York: Columbia University Press.

Morowitz, H. (2002). *The emergence of everything: How the world became complex*. Oxford, UK: Oxford University Press.

Moussaid, M., Helbing, D., & Theraulaz, G. (2011). How simple rules determine pedestrian behavior and crowd disasters. *Proceedings of the National Academy of Sciences*. Retrieved May 13, 2011, from http://www.pnas.org/cgi/doi/10.1073/pnas.1016507108.

National Association of Social Workers (2007). *Code of Ethics*. Retrieved April 29, 2011, from http://www.naswdc.org.

Neale, H. (1997). *Hockey Night in Canada*, June 7, 1997. Canadian Broadcasting Company: Toronto.

Nerney, T., Crowley, R., & Kappel, B. (1995). *An affirmation of community, a revolution of vision and goals: Creating a community to support all people including those with disabilities*. Durham: University of New Hampshire Institute on Disability.

NetLogo (2007). 3.1.4 NetLogo Users Manual. Retrieved May 4, 2010, from http://ccl.northwestern.edu/NetLogo/. Evanston, IL: Northwestern University.

Newman, M. E. J. (2010). *Networks: An introduction* (pp. 61–62). New York: Oxford University Press.

Norman, C. D., Best, A., Mortimer, S, Huerta, T., & Buchan, A. (2011). Evaluating the science of discovery in complex health systems. *American Journal of Evaluation, 32*(1), 70–84. doi: 10.1177/1098214010379038

Padgett, D. (2004). *The qualitative research experience* (pp. 1–18). Belmont, CA: Brooks/Cole.

Page, S. E. (2007). *The difference: How the power of diversity creates better groups, firms, schools, and societies*. Princeton, NJ: Princeton University Press.

Page, S. E. (2011). *Diversity and complexity*. Princeton, NJ: Princeton University Press.

Parker-Oliver, D., & Demiris, G. (2006). Social work informatics: A new specialty. *Social Work, 51*(2). 127–134.

Patton, M. Q. (2002). *Qualitative research and evaluation methods*, (pp. 123–126). Thousand Oaks, CA: Sage.

Patton, M. Q. (2008). *Utilization-focused evaluation* (4th ed.). Los Angeles: Sage.

Patton, M. Q. (2011). *Developmental evaluation: Applying complexity components to enhance innovation and use*. New York: Guilford Press.

Peterson, Martin (2009). *An introduction to decision theory*. Cambridge, UK: Cambridge University Press.

Pozatek, E. (1994). The problem of certainty: Clinical social work in the Postmodern Era. *Social Work, 39*(4), 396–403.

Pray, K. (2003). When is community organization social work practice? *Journal of Community Practice, 11*(3), 91–101.

Prigogine, I. (1996). *The end of certainty: Time, chaos, and the new laws of nature*. New York: Free Press.

Proehl, R. A. (2001). *Organizational change in the human services*. 76–80. Thousand Oaks, CA: Sage.

Pyles, L. (2009). *Progressive community organizing: A critical approach for a globalizing world*. New York: Routledge.

Reynolds, M. (2006). Evaluation based on critical systems heuristics. In B. Williams & I. Iman (Eds.), *Systems concepts in evaluation: An expert anthology* (pp. 101–121). Point Reyes, CA: EdgePress.

Rhee, Y. (2000). Complex systems approach to the study of politics. *Systems Research and Behavioral Science, 17*(6), 487–491.

Rossi, P. H., Lipsey, M. W., & Freeman, H. E. (2004) *Evaluation: A systematic approach* (7th ed). Thousand Oaks, CA: Sage.

Rubin, A., & Babbie, E. R. (2008). *Research methods in social work* (6th ed). Belmont, CA: Thomson.

Saari, E., & Kallio, K. (2011). Developmental impact evaluation for facilitating learning in innovation networks. *American Journal of Evaluation, 32*(2), 227–245.

Scearce, D., Kasper, G., & McLeod, H. (2010). Working wikily. *Stanford Social Innovation Review, Summer, 8*, 31–37.

Schelling, T. (1978). *Micromotives and macrobehavior*. New York: Norton.

Schreiner, M., & Sherraden, M. (2007). *Can the poor save? Savings and asset building in Individual Development Accounts [research monograph]*. New Brunswick, NJ: Transaction.

Senge, P. (2006). *The fifth discipline: The art and practice of the learning organization* (2nd ed.). New York: Doubleday.

Shafritz, J., and Ott, J. (1987). *Classics of organizational theory* (2nd ed., pp. 252–254). Chicago: Dorcey Press.

Shannon, C. E., & Weaver, W. (1949). *The mathematical theory of communication*. Urbana: University of Illinois Press.

Sherraden, M., & Barr, M.S. (2005). Institutions and inclusion in saving policy (pp. 286–315). In N. Retsinas & E. Belsky (Eds.), *Building assets, building credit: Creating wealth in low-income communities*. Washington: Brookings Institution Press.

Sterman, J. D. (2000). *Business dynamics: Systems thinking and modeling for a complex world*. New York: McGraw Hill.

Stevens, I., & Cox, P. (2008). Complexity theory: Developing new understandings of child protection in field settings and in residential child care. *British Journal of Social Work, 38*(7), 1320–1336.

Stevens, I., & Hassett, P. (2007) Applying complexity theory to risk in child protection practice. *Childhood, 14*(1), 129–146.

Steyaert, J., & Gould, N. (2009). Social work and the changing face of the digital divide. *British Journal of Social Work, 39*, 740–753.

Stringer, E. T., (1999). *Action research* (2nd ed.). Thousand Oaks, CA: Sage.

Strunk, G., Friedlmayer, S., & Brousek (2003). *A longitudinal analysis of long-term psychosocial care cases and a computer simulation game on social working practice. Research in the Field of Social Work*. Vienna: SraDt.

Surowiecki, J. (2004). *The wisdom of crowds*. New York: Random House.
Tabachnick, B., & Fidell, L. (2001). *Using multivariate statistics* (4th ed., pp. 17–30). Needham Heights, MA: Allyn & Bacon.
Taleb, N. N. (2010). *The black swan: The impact of the highly improbable*. New York: Random House.
Tenkasi, R. V., & Chesmore, M. C. (2003). Social networks and planned organizational change: The impact of strong network ties on effective change implementation and use. *The Journal of Applied Behavioral Science*, 39(3), 281–300.
Tierney, W. (2000). Undaunted courage: Life history and the postmodern challenge (pp. 537–565). In N. K. Denzin, & Y. S. Lincoln (Eds.), *Handbook of Qualitative Research* (2nd ed.). Thousand Oaks, CA: Sage.
Tracy E. M., & Brown, S. (2011). Social networks and social work practice. In F. J. Turner (Ed.), *Social work treatment: Interlocking approaches* (5th ed., pp. 447–459). New York: Oxford University Press.
Trevillon, S. (2000). Social work, social networks, and network knowledge. *British Journal of Social Work*, 30, 505–517.
Tripodi, T., Fellin, P., & Epstein, I. (1978). *Differential social program evaluation*. Itasca, IL: Peacock.
Turner, F. J. (2001). Theory development. In B. Thyer (Ed.), *The Handbook of Social Work Research Methods*. Thousand Oaks, CA: Sage.
Ulrich, W. (1996). *A primer to critical systems heuristics for action researchers*. Hull, UK: University of Hull.
van de Luitgaarden, G. M. J. (2009). Evidence-based practice in social work: Lessons from judgment and decision-making theory. *British Journal of Social Work*, 39, 243–260. doi: 10:1093/bjsw/bcm117
von Bertalanffy, L. (1968). *General system theory: Foundations, development, applications* New York: George Braziller.
Vygotsky, L. S. (1978). *Mind in society: The development of higher psychological processes*. Cambridge, MA: Harvard University Press.
Waldrop, M. M. (1992). *Complexity: The emerging science at the edge of chaos*. New York: Simon & Schuster.
Warren, K. (2008). Chaos theory and complexity theory. In T. Mizrahi & L. E. Davis (Eds.), *Encyclopedia of social work* (20th ed., pp. 227–233). Washington, DC: NASW Press.
Warren, K., Franklin, C., Streeter, C. L. (1998). New directions in systems theory: Chaos and complexity. *Social Work*, 43(4), 357–372.
Wasserman, S., & Faust, K. (1994). *Social network analysis: Methods and applications*. Cambridge, UK: Cambridge University Press.
Watts, D. J., & Strogatz, S. H. (1998). Collective dynamics of 'small world' networks. *Nature*, 393, 440–442.

References

Wiener, N. (1961). *Cybernetics: Or control and communication in the animal and the machine* (2nd ed.). Cambridge, MA: MIT Press.

Westley, F., Zimmerman, B., & Patton, M. Q. (2006). *Getting to maybe: How the world is changed*. Toronto: Random House Canada.

Wheatley, M. (1999). *Leadership and the new science: Discovering order in a chaotic world*. San Francisco: Berrett-Koehler.

Williams, B., & Imam, I. (2006). *Systems concepts in evaluation: An expert anthology* (pp. 3–16). Point Reyes, CA: EdgePress

Williams, B., & Hummelbrunner, R. (2011). *Systems concepts in action: A practitioner's toolkit*. Stanford, CA: Stanford University Press.

Woehle, R. (2007). Complexity theory, nonlinear dynamics, and change augmenting systems theory. *Advances in Social work, 8*(1), 141–151.

Woehle, R., Jones, G., Baker, T., & Piper, M. (2009). Theory and modeling of emergent behaviors: The effects of intervention on social and cultural capital. *Social Development Issues, 31*(2), 43–56.

Wolf-Branigin, K., & Wolf-Branigin, M., Culver, J.D. & Welch, K. (2012). Can travel training services save public transportation agencies money? *TR News*, January-February (278), 36–38.

Wolf-Branigin, M. (2006). Self-organization in housing choices of persons with disabilities. *Journal of Human Behavior in the Social Environment, 13*(4), 25–35.

Wolf-Branigin, M. (2009). Applying complexity and emergence in social work education. *Social Work Education: The International Journal, 28*, 115–127.

Wolf-Branigin, M., & Duke, J. (2007). Spiritual involvement as a predictor to completing a Salvation Army substance abuse treatment program. *Researchon Social Work Practice, 17*(2), 239–245. doi: 10.1177/1049731506294373

Wolf-Branigin, M., & LeRoy, B. (2004). Designing accessible managed care services for people with physical disabilities: Consumer suggestions within an emergent design process. *Journal of Social Work in Disability and Rehabilitation, 3*(3), 3–16. doi:10.1300/J198v03n03_02

Wolf-Branigin, M., LeRoy, B., and Miller, J. (2001). Physical inclusion of people with developmental disabilities: An evaluation of the Macomb-Oakland Regional Center. *American Journal on Mental Retardation, 106*(4), 368–375.

Wolf-Branigin, M., Schuyler, V., & White, P. (2007). Improving quality of life and career readiness of adolescents with disabilities: Experiences from the Adolescent Employment Readiness Center. *Research on Social Work Practice, 17*(3), 324–333. doi: 10.1177/1049731506295623

Wolfram, S. (2002). *A new kind of science*. Champaign, IL: Wolfram Media.

Wooldridge, R. (1981). *New Directions for program evaluation: Evaluation of complex systems*, 10 (pp. vii–viii). San Francisco: Wiley.

Zimmerman, B. (2000). *Examples of wicked questions*. Bordentown, NJ: Plexus Institute. http://www.plexusinstitute.org/.

Index

Agent, 9, 13–15, 174
Agent-based modeling (ABM), 2–7, 30, 33–34, 41, 45, 51, 82, 94–113, 114–130, 174
Boolean logic, 62, 67, 174
Boundaries, 10, 25, 32, 36–37, 47, 134, 145, 169, 174

Cellular automata, 67, 69, 92, 99, 115–116, 118–119, 174
Chaos theory, 11, 19, 38, 95, 174
Complex adaptive systems, 1, 8, 37, 134, 174
Complexity theory, 1–14, 175
Complex systems, 1–18, 25–28, 175
Computation theory, 67–69, 176
Convergence, 175
Cybernetics, 81, 82, 86, 175

Description length, 12, 175
Decision theory, 62–63, 175
Developmental evaluation, 22, 44, 54–55, 133, 137, 147–148, 175
Diverse heuristics, 22, 24, 78, 91, 135, 137, 175
Diverse perspectives, 5, 7, 21–22, 24, 27, 30, 50, 78–79, 83, 137, 175
Dynamical systems theory, 175

Ecosystems theory, 7, 17, 70, 175
Edge of Chaos, 19, 78, 91, 175
Effective complexity, 11, 12, 176
Emergence/emergent behavior, 3–5, 9, 20, 24–27, 33, 38–39, 44, 48, 74, 176
Entanglement, 6, 176
Entropy, 42
Evolutionary computation, 176

Fractal, 136, 142, 144

General systems theory, 7, 9, 10, 17, 70, 82, 86, 176
Groupthink, 137, 176

In silico, 14, 141, 176
Interconnectedness, 6–7, 10, 16, 33, 41, 64, 79, 95, 142, 176

Kolmogorov complexity, 11, 12, 176

Meme, 176

Negative feedback, 18, 38, 42, 117–118
Network analysis, 10, 16, 30, 51, 64, 73, 75, 138
Network thinking, 16
Neural networks, 16, 138, 176

195

Niche construction, 22, 177
Nonlinearity, 3, 38–39, 70, 177

Positive feedback, 18, 37–38, 42, 117–118
Power laws, 55, 121, 135–136, 169, 177

Quantum mechanics, 3, 14, 19

Random graphs, 177

Scalability, 6, 24, 78, 135, 167, 169
Self-organizing behavior, 13, 28, 29, 39, 44, 69–71, 137, 177
Self-similarity, 7, 23, 78, 135, 142–143, 177
Sensitivity to initial conditions, 19, 34–35, 38, 177
Simple rules, 12–13, 26, 30, 64, 89, 99, 115, 125, 177

Simulation, 7, 14, 74, 90, 98, 105, 122, 138
Small-world networks, 55, 98, 177
Social innovation, 80, 146
Spatial analysis, 10, 51, 56–58, 62, 68, 87, 96, 120, 177
Spatial autocorrelation, 37, 39, 57, 66–67, 87–88, 177
Statistical complexity, 11–12, 178
Systems thinking, 8, 10, 25

Unintended consequences, 125, 178

Validation, 121–122, 178
Verification, 120–121, 178

Wicked questions, 144, 178
Wisdom of crowds, 22, 24, 27, 134, 178

Printed in Great Britain
by Amazon